Part 1

It is safe to say that we are the creators of our reality as well as being in complete control over what we choose to excel in. In many circumstances it very common this day and age that you have grown up in a single parent family. This may limit the amount of opportunity to have a good family image to portray as you decide to have a family of your own. The rising percentage of this epidemic will continue to expand as long as the basic laws of life are not tended to. This is to say that the abundance of the people that do not caress the factors involved in the development of a human being in this case being their child, the statistical percentage of crime, poverty, teen pregnancy, and etcetera, will continue to grow at an alarming rate.

There still is a large portion of individuals that have beaten the odds due to their initial circumstances. The amount of women that have decided to go to college has risen in comparison to the past as well. It is a very critical thing that we challenge ourselves on an everyday basis to become and achieve a certain level of understanding on the elements of an economic future that lie in our future. This can only be done by making an individual effort to change ourselves and others in our immediate vicinity.

Constructing your reality is all you can do to achieve your desires. Changing the world is something you can only achieve by setting an example for others to follow. After this example setting process, which will indefinitely last beyond your own personal lifetime, entire Mecca's and civilizations will change at a very slow but sure path towards the unity of all in decades and centuries to follow. This process can only be undergone by one person at a time that is why the importance of nurturing our children throughout their young lives is a must if we wish to turn the tables on humanity. The convenience of doing so in the youth of our children can only build a picture in one's mind of what the future may entail.

Understanding that our minds, bodies, and spirits can only operate on a well distinguished frequency when they are in sync with our health is what brings an optimal level of enlightenment and self reflection to our total existence. To understand these basic principles, you may only perceive them on an individual basis if you wish to embark on this path of total consciousness and righteousness. You may participate only if you choose to separate yourself from the barrier that you have put in front of yourself and to guard from the pain and frustrations that everyday life may bring. This so-called barrier is a source of protection that the human species produces in their mind to manipulate their thinking in way in which would block out certain emotions to keep them at ease from a particular element of emotion. If you want to break down these barriers in your mind, it is essential that you open yourself.

Open yourself in a way that you can expend any type of emotion that you are holding in, emotions of when you were young, emotions of when people hurt you, things that you have held in, things that are creating these barriers that are keeping you from becoming more open. Honesty can be the single most effective tool in getting out these emotions. When you are honest, you have the ability to say and do all that is in accordance with the elevated frequencies that you want to operate on. This in most cases means that you don't hold anything in any longer. If you hold these energies internally, it will literally eat you up inside. Stress, by itself, can tear you apart on the inside, as well as anxiety, anger, jealousy; these particular emotions weigh heavily on your health in addition to your outer circumstances and the way that you live your life.

Hate and resentment can only bring hate and resentment towards you. If you express love and joy, love and joy will come to you. In other words, what you reap in life, you will sow unto others. To every action there is an opposite reaction. Like looking in the mirror, what you see is what you get, and even what you think about yourself can distract you from thinking anything positive outwardly. What you think about yourself goes hand and hand with the way you feel about others.

If you think you are ugly and whatever else it is that you call yourself that is what others will see in you. But if you tell yourself you are beautiful and special, that is exactly what other people will see in you. You must always love and care for yourself, if you do not, nobody will care for you either, in fact, you cannot expect anyone to.

Put yourself in the other person's shoes; for example: you keep trying to love this person but they keep shutting you out, you try to do things for them, but they just don't seem to appreciate anything you do. It begins to get frustrating and you then decide that you will no longer take the effort, leaving them in their own world of sadness. They complain about this they complain about that, and now that you are not constantly trying to be nice to them anymore, they are complaining about you.

From an outsider's perspective, you can now see how self pity can wear on the people around you and how self hate can just make things worse than they really are towards your inner and outer being. It is safe to say that in the event of life, how you tend to do anything reflects how you do everything. You can always start doing things differently, which means that you can start to get better results.

People have the tendency to blame others for their particular set of circumstances which can also be defined by the above paragraph. For instance, I'm sure you have heard someone say, I can't do this because blank said that. These people are blocking their own progression by blaming others. Until you start taking responsibility for your own actions, you will find that you will find yourself getting nowhere. Nobody but yourself can take responsibility for your actions. If you have successfully blamed someone for something that you have done in the past, and got away with it, look forward to having the same thing reciprocate towards you.

Life and existence is a flow of energy that coexists. Think of everything you do and say as being a boomerang; it will always come back to you. Until you realize the ever powerful magnitude of your thoughts and actions, you will remain a leaf in the wind with no definite course.

Put yourself in a position where everything you do and say are the tools that you use to manifest what you want. If you choose bad actions and thoughts you will manifest what comes with that set of introspection and vice versa.

Integrity and the ability to act on what you say is a very good way to learn how to follow through, when you follow through the energy that you have composed in doing what you say you were going to do actually circulates instead of being blocked. When the energy is blocked, the energy stays within and builds up to be a bigger and more detouring energy which grows into a very constant state of procrastination. With this ever building energy of procrastination it will take twice as much work to get to the state of integrity that you are looking for.

Lack of integrity can cause relationships to go bad. People that make plans and don't follow through with them, people that say one thing and do another thing, these are the people that I am speaking of in this case.

We have all had this happen to us and I am sure you didn't like it. It is also safe to say that some of us have also had a lack of integrity at a certain times of our lives ourselves. To administer the correct action, it is best to rely on the truth and honesty when dealing with integrity based situations. Telling someone how it is honestly is always the best method of sealing the cracks in a particular situation. If you must partake in an action that you have planned and you have fallen out of the grasps of commitment, it is wise that you advise others of what it is that has changed your line of action. To mend all loose ends it an easy way to keep a positive energy flowing.

A great way to get in tune with your higher self is to take a visit into nature, even a breath of fresh air can be a very exhilarating and crucial part in getting back in touch with yourself. Within all of us, are the elements of our soul and we must exercise our inner self whenever possible.

Our inner self must be nurtured as much as possible. It is very easy for exterior elements to damper on our minds and our souls on a regular basis. If you live a very busy lifestyle, dedicate an hour a week to yourself. Take a walk, go to the park, go on a hike; anything to free your energy from the ordinary things that you may do on a day to day basis. The more time you can dedicate to yourself the faster you may deploy the anxiety and feelings of tenseness that you hold within.

Depleting these energies brings you in touch with yourself so it is a crucial counterpart in the self healing process. There are other forms of dissipating this energy, such as; Yoga, Pilates, running and other forms of exercise. I still suggest that you spend some time in complete silence with nature as well; it will be more beneficial spiritually in the long run.

Past emotions and feelings are things that we must really focus on releasing. The build-up of such energies is nothing more than a weakness that we must find an answer for and believe me there is an answer to all the questions that we hold within. When you acknowledge the problem, the answers will manifest only if you seek them. The collections of past emotions that most of us hold inside are only a safety barrier to keep us from getting hurt as we have in the past.

When we are children it is easy to get scolded, abused, and hurt in many other ways, mainly because we are a very easy target for these unforeseen events. Being a victim of such events at a time when we are at the height of our learning, these feelings and emotions have the tendency to stay dormant. Subconsciously these feelings and emotions become complacent and mundane in our everyday lives leading to the way we react to just about everything. These are the most difficult emotions to release. Being the victim at such a young age, you have to recognize that the people who have abused and hurt you were going through their own life traumas. The things that you have felt guilty about in your childhood are their problems and whether it has left a scar on whom you are today or not, it may not be easy to choke up the forgiveness. A good way of letting go is to separate yourself from how weak it has made you feel, and think about how strong you will become having been a survivor of such an event.

If you keep looking back, you will always stay back. If you look forward, you will move forward. In the event that you decide to move forward, you will rapidly see how you were acting in the past and how it was affecting you. In a timely matter even the thoughts of such events will dissolve in your mind and instead of being a constant reminder of your past it will remain a footprint in the mountain of life you have climbed.

Love will always be the strongest energy of compassion and with it you must realize that the people that hurt you must have been hurt too when they were a child. Abuse; in many ways is a learned behavior and with that in mind, visualize the perpetrator getting abused and think of why they have become the person that they are. In many ways, the perpetrator has kept the emotion fresh in their mind of when they had too been abused. The only difference between the perpetrator and the person you are going to become is that you are going to end this cycle of abuse, and by converting this energy into a positive, you again can have the openness as you once did when you were a child. These emotions could have played a huge role as to how you handled your relationships up this point.

You may now look back and learn from you past relationship errors and see how the abuse had caused a negative pattern in your life as well. Ending this complex destructive pattern can mean the difference in your family life as well as your future relationships that follow; the final destination of this negative energy pattern has been smothered out, and will no longer affect you or your family as long as your realization of such an idle energy exists.

To become one with your inner self means that you must release yourself and become one with everything. You are; the trees that blow in the wind, the air, the sky, the feeling you get when you love someone, the sun, the stars. You are me, and I am you; we are one. To completely understand this you must release yourself. What is it that makes you any different from anyone else? What your mind perceives is your realization, and what you realize is yourself. What you are is everyone and what everyone is, you are as well.

*

There is nothing more common than someone who travels half way up the mountain and then decides to turn around. Realizing that the events that may change your mind about pushing forward are the things that make you stronger and more agile in completing your ascent towards what it is that you are aspiring for. By stopping your positive flow of energy, you are in fact telling the universe that you gave up, and when you tell the universe that you have given up, it will always give you another challenge that is equally as challenging.

Life itself is a mountain that must be climbed and in doing so you will face the exact same barriers on your uphill battle as mentioned before. Everything you do, say, and express outwardly are also in rhythm with the circumstances that affect your uphill climb. Thoughts and actions are the tools that you use to climb this mountain. Some may have the ability to use these tools more efficiently than others and some may appear to use these tools such as a caveman in the early stages in human civilization. No matter what stage you are in on your uphill ascent, the way you use these tools depend on how you have chosen to educate yourself on certain elements of life. Being open to advice is one way of doing so. Choosing which advice to take can be hard, but if you use your intuition and gut feeling while choosing, your selection process will be more efficient than if you were to second guess the first thing that came to mind.

Letting what is happening right now get to you, can affect you very negatively when it could be a virtuous moment in your life. Putting too much weight on what is going on right now can only detour you from the proper path, displacing your advancement until a later date. We all want such a process to flow very effortlessly and at ease with our state of mind, but it will only flow at that level if you live for tomorrow and not for the present moment.

This is not to say that you shall not enjoy the right here and now in your life, but rather use now as key to make your future more in tune with what you really want. You have to realize that everything happens for a reason and there is a divine purpose for every individual experience in your life whether or not it seems good or bad at first sight. Every experience that you have when you are alive is in perfect sequential order; the universe is fluid and will always operate in perfect order as it should. Knowing that everything is taking place in perfect order, you shall not bear too much of your energy to any particular event; letting your life unfold the way it is supposed to and not dwelling on a particular past event or a bad event taking place can speed up your advancement process.

In life there will always be events that will test your courage as well as your ability to keep composure. These events only have a meaning because you have made a definition for them. By understanding that we do not live in a world of duality and in fact we live in a world of universal harmony, you will learn to appreciate every event as a gift of God whether if it seems good or bad. There will always be something good out of each thing that is defined as bad and there will always be something bad out of each thing that is defined as good; not necessarily by you but by the multitude of people that experience the event. If you are the only person who is affected by a certain event, you hold the definition as to what it means to you. In a group setting, each person will interpret the event differently.

In a world that is completely reflective and fluid in energy flow, we will always be in control of defining every experience in our own given context. By having this ability, you must keep in perspective that the definition you give it is what will affect your future and what outcome of each situation may be. You can turn a negative experience into a positive experience if you choose to learn from it instead of letting it defeat you.

Like a race car driver on a track with a lot of turns, you must keep your hands on the wheel at all times. If you let go of the wheel, you will crash and have to make some repairs before you can get back into the race. I use this analogy only to make an example on how the process actually works. If you over analyze things they become too complicated and by using that as an analogy, it gives you a visual of what may occur if you do not keep in control of your life. Some people spend most of their lives making repairs only to crash once again. Some people crash and never put time into making repairs only leaving them in the same spot for an extended period of time, and they live a very short life as a result of it. Hopefully that removes the complexity of taking these steps forward and gives you a much easier explanation of how this process takes place.

Have you ever wondered why some people are unaffected by such events that would affect you greatly? It may be because they are in harmony with themselves or it may be an experience that they have already experienced prior. It having been an experience that they had experienced prior, they have found a certain set of strengths that have empowered them. You will find strength through experience if you choose to learn. If you play the martyr and complain outwardly to attain pity from your peers and immediate social surroundings, you will become consumed by what could have been something that empowered you.

You can always turn a good into a bad or a bad into a good. Has something bad ever happened to you? If you said yes then you must realize that it always follows with a positive. For instance you are reading this book right now, and it will help you reflect on all those negative experiences that led you to this point. If those negative experiences never happened you not have been interested in reading this book.

You can create a very powerful system that empowers you each day. Start by letting go of your emotional attachments. Love, peace and happiness are the only human emotions that are pure and always positive. Hate, anger, and jealousy are the most humanly destructive energies that exist in man today. Say the word love and notice how it makes you feel. Now say the word hate and see how it makes you feel. Every word holds energy; it can be an empowering word or a very limiting word. The words you choose to use define you, and tell the world what you are about is how your personal life is defined. Are you good, or are you bad?

Learning how to cope with everyday problems can be a very arduous task, or it can be a very easy way to learn and grow. Through these events you will learn but only if you choose to. Don't let your problems become bigger than you. If the problem seems too big to tackle on your own, it is always reassuring to ask someone that you can trust in for a simple solution. You will find that some people have been through those certain problems, and know just the right way to solve them.

Being committed to what you want to do will always be the light at the end of the tunnel. If you do not have a point B or a goal to achieve you are leaving an unclear message for the universe, and it will not direct you in a definite direction. Have you ever felt lost? That is the result of not having short and long term goals set. Setting goals should be like brushing your teeth or taking a shower, it should become a very normal occurrence in your everyday life. As soon as you wake each morning, you should make goals for the day that will create a vehicle to your short term goals.

Your daily goals will lead to the success of your short term goals, your short term goals will lead to the success of your long term goals. It might take you a thousand short term goals to get to your long term goals and it could take ten, but being active in the manifestation process means that you must always set goals. There will be more failure than success along the way sometimes and it is completely normal to have that amount of failure. Successful people learn to become ok with constant failure; and with that failure, you will become stronger and more efficient along the way. If you let the little failures get to you, you will have little success.

This all has something to do with taking risks. For the most part the larger the risk the larger the size of the reward will be. Having faith in the achievement and the proper course of actions is all you need to attain success. Even when you fail, the continuance of your faith must still exist. You may have taken the wrong course of action, but with the failure of your first attempt, you will have insight on what you could have done different. Now it's a whole new ballgame, you at least have another piece of the puzzle. You still may fail again, and again after that, but each time you learn a valuable lesson on your approach to what it is that your heart desires. This process works on every aspect in life and if you practice this process you will surly find what it is you seek.

On the other hand if you choose to never take any risks, never choose to learn, grow, you will basically become another person that is adrift in their life, living on the roller coaster of happiness and sadness.

We live in a fear based society and what you learn in school, TV, the radio, all has to do with how happy or how fearful you are. Advertising and news is based on the psychological patterns of the human mind. Our personal existence is based on how we feel about certain thing. Everything that we see and do has a feeling attached to it. Every object in our reality has a certain meaning and or energy tied to it that we have created for it. All these meanings that we have created are all in a spectrum of energy which is either negative, positive, or anywhere in between. From the power of thought, we can transform or redefine the meaning of any such energy. We can transform anything we want with reactive thought. Reactive thought is when you have the ability to create or redefine the particular energy that is attached to an event or circumstances. Being able to transform the definition, you can create a meaning that has less negative impact on your nervous system which can help your anxiety and the ability to analyze situations with ease and control. What this means is that you can make conversions in your own universal reality. When you make those changes your existence will fit the mold of your mental infrastructure, giving you the ability to have and do what you want. We are all composed of energy and in the spectrum of energy in our infinite universe, we can construct any compose any element to what it is that we so desire. Our inner world can manipulate our outer world in certain increments and in that process is when we have the ability to manifest our desires. These small increments of life and reality manipulation, give us the opportunity to construct favorable short term circumstances. Using the application of this process is how you can make a difference. This all does not happen in a day, week, month or year; it happens at the rate of speed at which you have the wherewithal to accommodate into you present situation. Like I said before, you must work your way up the ladder of your short to long term goals. Write these goals down somewhere where you can see them on a regular basis i.e. journal, notebook, background on your computer, there are many ways to help you with the manifestation. Stop what you are doing right now and focus on what it is you really want. Do you want a big car, fancy home, that perfect someone? These are all questions that we must ask ourselves in addition to a million other unique things that you want in your life. All this has to start with goal setting and working on those goals one at a time. When you begin to do this, you start to gather these goals at a more rapid pace. Life is filled with an endless amount of possibilities and if you don't particularly believe that you can attain what it is that you want, you probably can't. Without believing that you can gain what you want in life, there is very little that you can achieve. Believe that you are the master of your life and you will become a molder and maker of your personal existence. Feel as though you are the creator of the universe, have a mental capacity that allows you to think, believe, and materialize anything that you desire.

Consider yourself as a very flexible and versatile being that can morph into any particular setting. How we structure our energy to match any such environment depends on the amount of faith and belief in commanding the reality of our lives. Faith to me means no that matter what is happening or is about to happen can affect your decision on what it is that you are trying to accomplish.

Only fear can make you resist what it is that you desire, no not fear anything; fear is the most powerful weakness that exists and with it you cannot move forward. Stand up face front to all your fears, look all your fears in the eye and know that if you back down, you will be beaten, and if you are beaten, you have lost. The smallest source of fear you have in your body only exists because you let it. Breaking out of your comfort zone gives you the ability to grow. As a plant needs water to grow, you cannot grow without watering your root. Fear inhibits the watering of your roots, and blocks the flow of positive energy. Have no fear; take your life by the horns with positive energy, a kind heart and the ability to block your fears with faith and belief in yourself and you will be able to accomplish all things that you have not had the wherewithal to achieve prior to the understanding of this process. Set yourself free from your self-constructed barriers and live the life that the universe has intended for you.

Part 2

In order to truly move on in your life, from past life patterns, you must have the ability to forgive. Forgiveness is when you emotionally let go of a certain issue that had prior affected your life negatively. Forgiving someone for a certain thing they did to you, or forgiving yourself for something you did to yourself is one of the most releasing things that can take place in one's life. Having the ability to forgive is part of us which is not always the most active part of our conscious effort, but something that we must act upon.

It may be the hardest thing in the world to come to terms with someone and actually forgive them for something that they did to you or even something that they did in spite of you. Even know it may be the toughest thing to do, it may be the most rewarding thing that you can do, releasing both bad feelings for another and releasing bad energy that is contained in your being. I find that if you have the unwillingness to forgive someone, you become almost as bad as the perpetrator.

When you are unwilling to forgive, you harness the energy that was emitted from the spite, envy, and anger at the time of the fallout. When you keep these negative energies contained within your being, you hold all the emotional energy that occurred at the point of the incident. Now, look back and find all the times that you became hateful and full of spite as result of what someone else did to you. Now think of how all those experiences created a wall of some sort, blocking you from having any more experiences that were similar to those of the past. Think of how your life would be if you had forgiven these people for what they have done instead of holding all the negativity inside. When you lack the will to forgive, you become a ball of anger, spite, and envy that is ready to act just as though you were the person who hurt you or your feelings.

This is not to say that you must actually forgive someone face to face, you may only do that on your own terms if you allow yourself, but it is necessary and more important that you forgive someone in your heart. Forgiving those who have done the most awful things is a way of releasing the most awful emotions.

You may also be the person who has done something bad or unrighteous, and you also must find a way in your heart to forgive yourself for what you have done. This may be a bit more difficult, especially if it has noticeable affected the ones that you love. The feelings of uneasiness are always present when you are around the people that you have affected. You may hold a certain amount of self hatred, this can lead to many forms of self-abuse including, drug abuse, alcoholism, and so on and so forth. You may always come to terms with this self hatred, but only if you have the will to let go of the discomfort that you have held in for so long. Clearing your mind is a great way to find who you really are underneath all the built-up layers of self dissatisfaction that you have built up. If you continue to drown all your sorrows with the drugs and alcohol, you may never come to terms with your not so beneficial past experiences. Drugs and alcohol are foreign substances that alter the way you think. They inhibit the ability to focus on reality and the underlying issues that you are trying to disguise with the substance. It may take a long time to reach complete clarity as result of your sobriety, and in some cases, maybe even longer depending on your level of addiction. When you have met the level of clarity that is crucial for self-cleansing, you may now dig up all the elements of your past that you have held in your heart up to that point. You must leave your comfort zone and enter a new reality by stepping out of the box that you have stayed in for so long, and in the process, you must release everything, not just a couple of things. When you have had the ability to do so, you will find a lot of interconnectivity between all the issues. Some things held-in may have had the ability to stack up, due to one particular event, leading to a set of actions thereafter.

The containment of feelings that have led you to a state of not forgiving others is primarily a self-built wall of protection that does not allow others to hurt you. As the rule of reciprocity states; you reap what you sow, what you do unto others, will be unto you. Many different philosophies of the subject suggest the same thing, including quantum physics. This is to say that if you do not forgive others, others will not forgive you. If you do not love yourself, others will not love you. The mechanics of these laws adhere to everything in life and it is something that you cannot fight.

You can choose to take another route, but in the end, you will always receive the same results. The constant flow of positive energy flow will always allow positive things to enter your life. You can't have something that you don't completely agree with. If there is a bit of disbelief in the thing that you want and need in your life, you will not have the ability to manifest what's in your heart.

There are many different ways to forgive, one of the most difficult, is forgiving others for what they have done to you. That is, bar none, the most difficult of all. Some of the things that were done have scarred you emotionally, mentally and in some cases physically. It being one of the most difficult ways of forgiveness means that it is the most beneficial to your being and the most powerful in the self-healing process.

If there were a method of forgiving, I believe that you must heal yourself by understanding that what has happened or what you have gone through, was a temporary event, it does not define who you are or who you will be in the future. Some people can never fathom it in their heart to forgive those who have hurt them. You must end the cycle of this by letting go and letting things be. There is no need to re-live the event every day in your head. In some ways, the constant recollections of these thoughts have arrested your development in more than one way, leaving you powerless and empty as a person.

Dissolving these thoughts consist of a clear-headed resolution that can only be achieved by visualizing how these events have affected you and by skimming over how they have made you feel in the past. Take a stand; use your inner emptiness to defeat the feelings in your heart and by doing so you may now move forward in many ways.

Why have you let these things destroy your existence up until this point? How could you carry the weight of someone else's problems on your shoulders? Why have you let these things conquer you? You're probably saying to yourself, "That's a good question". Stomp out those realities by understanding that the perpetrator was the person with the problem and that they were the people with the issues, not you. Everything that humans do, are a collection of learned behaviors that consist of the things that they themselves learned as a child. The most powerful time of cognitive growth, is when we are children. Think of the perpetrator as a child being abused, they did not know the difference between what is good and what is bad while they were at that age, the abuse then became something that is normal to the child, hence the ability to commit such abuse as they grow older. I know this puts a different spin on the subject, but in reality, this is why the abuse continues to persist. You can probably continue going up the chain and find that their forefathers and mothers were a victim of the same elements. The reason that you must forgive in your heart those who have trespassed against you, is because the feelings of hate and resentment stay fresh in your heart as did the perpetrator from their experience of abuse.

These things may have left you powerless and at the mercy of others until today. I want you to let go, let go of the pain that you feel in your heart; forgive, forget, and let be.

Life is a learning experience and you cannot control the outer circumstances that have lain upon you, the only thing that you can control is your inner feelings and the way that they either benefit you or affect you negatively in the spectrum of life.

Achieve your destinies, fulfill your dreams, let your aspirations blossom and let your life flourish as you forgive yourself and others and let the past slip away each day, you are the grand creator of your reality and the possessor of a beautiful soul, let it shine.

*

A helping hand is all you need sometimes to make it through a tough situation. Someone is not always there, therefore you must become self sufficient. In the instance I'm speaking of, a helping hand is defined as someone or something that can assist you on your own growth or learning curve; this may or may not be a person but can also be an experience, a book, a seminar, or just the power of the universe alone.

Experiencing life at your own pace is all that you can do, and these elements that help you on your way can pop up at any time; being aware of these things is all that you have to do as an individual to progress at the specific pace that you are accustomed to or that you are prescribed to by the universe.

Being open to whatever is coming your way, as well as being analytic to these things is the key to noticing what is helping you or not. By being open and not shutting out everything that comes your way, you can find a lot of different pieces to your individual puzzle. In these moments, you will feel as though you have had an epiphany, and at that second you will know that the helping hand has just reached out.

Everything happens for a reason, and these hands of guidance can be the single most effective way understanding your purpose. If you open your eyes and ears, you will find out that they are all around you. If you find yourself asking for help in a state of weakness and you are wondering why you have not manifested the answers to your questions, it is because you must seek inward with strength and perseverance. If you are asking outwardly with weakness, you will not receive the answers no matter how hard you try. This is why the weak willed person tends to get weaker the more circumstance that knocks at their door.

We have all stumbled to that point at one time or another in our life and it is always a great thing that we can change with every new day and mold ourselves into the person that we want to be at the pace at which we feel is comfortable.

Consider the growth rate of a human being as a statistic like that of a percentage of some degree. If you grow at the average rate of others with equal circumstances, you are not quite making an impact on yourself or unto others. I think it is always important to shine with goodness and bliss, and the energy you emit only be well perceived by others. Think of it like; what you reap, you also sow and this is how you act and feel to others. The more emotion that you keep tethered within, the longer it will take to come into terms with yourself.

If your vehicle of choice is learning about spirituality, choose to learn about spirituality until it is to you at a great level of perception. We often tend to want to know about everything and wind up getting our wires crossed. I think the best method of nurturing your newly growing roots, would be to learn one thing at a time, maybe several different sources.

Don't take everything you read as gospel, but pick and choose the bits of information that resonate with you the most. You will see, once you have studied different philosophies or theories that there are a lot of commonalities. You will also find more pieces to the puzzle i.e. missing bits of information that complete a certain set of thoughts that you have pondered in the past.

With learning about life, spirituality, and the ultimate level of wellness you will become more apt to passing this information on to others. There are certain methods of doing so, but it is more of an example setting process than pushing information down a person's throat type of situation.

Before you get even near that point you will come to the fork in the road whether you want to do this or not. It takes unbreakable patience, extreme perseverance, and a very high level of determination, depending on how far you are from where you want to be.

There will come a time in this process that some of the people you love will taunt you and say your different, your being fake, you're not being yourself, as a result to you self betterment. At this time you will find out who to break communication with and who to continue engaging yourself with. It will be family members, it will be friends. The level of intellect that you now possess will now supersede that of the people that you used to communicate with. Some of them will like the new you and may decide to follow your lead; some will continue their ignorance and spite towards your newly enlightened self.

This separation is a very crucial thing; the longer you hang out waiting for these people to transform, the longer it will take for your own change, and sometimes this lingering of negativity can actually bring you back to the point where you started and you may even quit the process.

This is all not to say that you would completely separate yourself from these people, this is to say that you would separate your energy from theirs. If this person is not in your immediate household or vicinity, you can simply stop hanging around with them. If you communicate with these people via the telephone, you may decide to stop engaging with them as soon as they start to become negative. You can only change yourself and you will only become very impatient with those you are trying to change, primarily because they must want change before they can change. These people might come around again, but only once they see the result that you have shown. You can only be an example setter in this particular situation.

"Negativity is like a cold. It slowly enters your being without notice, increasing in intensity and becomes contagious if not treated. The medicine for each strain of negativity also differs i effectiveness, finding the proper dose of that cure may also be a tough task as well. To find th remedy, you must seek inward to get a diagnosis. Once you have found the root issue to your negativity, you must get some rest and direct all your energy towards repairing your slowly weakening spirit, and in due time, with constant effort and an open mind, your negativity will be wiped out. Maintain a healthy mind with healthy food, thoughts, and people; otherwise you will always be trying to find the right elixir to maintain that positivity." ~Will Barnes

Only when you have a firm set of feet on the ground that is evident to the people that you are encompassed by, you may then be an example to others who seek enlightenment. You may wish to join a non-profit group that helps others in need if helping others is what you want to do.

Whether you just want to help yourself, or you want to help others, it is always beneficial to you and the world around you. The energy that you will now hold will resonate with the people that surround you regardless of whether you are trying to or not.

Let's say that you live in a less desirable neighborhood and the people in your area are negative and overwhelming to be in presence of; I suggest that you do your best at finding a new place to live no matter what it takes. As long as your positive energy flows, the universe can only be on your side in the event of trying to find a new place to live. Do not doubt that anything is possible and if you ask, you shall receive, but only with true faith. This may not happen overnight, in most cases it will not, if fact it may take a week, a month, a year. Don't fall short of your goal; keep the vision of where you will be in your mind no matter what stands in your path.

You cannot completely change and you cannot expect to; there is a bit of originality in everyone that you must hang on to keep your character. It may be all you have left, if not, you will indefinitely build a newer more fantastic you. There are bits and pieces of your past that will stick around, but those things that have weakened you in the past are now going to be the glue that strengthens you. Having turned all your weaknesses into your strengths, you will become a powerhouse at life and there will be nothing to stand in your way of who you want to be.

Who do you want to be? How high do you want to go? Where do you want to travel to? The answer is simple. The choice is yours, and when you decide to make this choice with unbreakable faith and conviction, the universe will pull together all the strength that you have put into this thought or group of thoughts, and what you want will be showered upon you in accordance and consistent with the energy you put into it.

Just like a professional athlete; you must practice every day until you become very good. And when you become very good, you must still practice every day. It is a process in which you shall never decide to quit, a process that should become a mundane activity in your daily life.

When you have become a master, you may then decide to enlighten others who seek spiritual and physical attainment. Needless to say, it is evident that it is our will as an enlightened individual, is to help others that are in need.

Anything you do to help others aids with the reciprocation of energy. Almost like a contagion i.e. a cold, a disease, etcetera; if you help someone, the likeliness that they will help someone else will increase. If you spread kindness in works the same way.

For example; have you ever had the feeling that you wanted to help someone, and the only reason that you made an attempt to do so is because someone helped you similarly in the past? I think we all have, and if you have not, today is always a good day to start.

All this is to practice your selflessness and if you do your part as an individual, the flow of such energy in the world will be more prominent in your reality leading to better relationships and the ability to become more active in your community. Energy goes a long way when it is properly honed in a certain direction.

To be at one, is to be at one with the universe, and to be at one with the universe is to be at one with self. To a certain degree, it is our primary purpose as a human being other than procreation, to make affect others lives. You can either affect their lives positively or negatively, make your choice as which it is going to be.

In our lives we are always seeking better jobs, better lifestyles, and self betterment. Unfortunately we try to do that by focusing on our selves ultimately. The thing is, we are not here in this world alone, and we do not advance successively without others in our lives. We must attain a balance between ourselves and others to achieve outward achievement. Although it is crucial that we retain a high level of self sufficiency, we become more efficient as a person if we share our knowledge and helping hand to others.

Have you met a person who will not let you help them? Have you met a person who thinks they know it all? These people tend to carry these characteristics in everything they do. These people are usually the same people that complain that nobody ever helps them. This is another example of how you treat others you will be treated equally in return. If that person happens to be you, you now know how and why those particular circumstances have become a large part of why you have received those results in the past.

What you define as beauty or success is defined and perceived only in your eyes to your individual reality so it is pertinent that you judge things very lightly. Having a certain definition or judgment to each and everything you come in contact with will give you a certain set of results each time you decide to judge. It is like you are painting a picture, in your mind you have already described your finished product, and all you have to do is fill in the rest with your thoughts. If you have a set of limiting thoughts, you will get limited results. If you have an open mind to every person, place, or thing, you are certain to get a different set of results each time. You create the story of each individual experience that you encounter each day. With a healthy mind, you will have healthy thoughts and a healthy lifestyle. With bad thoughts, and bad health, you will live an unhealthy lifestyle; a perfect example of the domino effect.

Our minds, bodies, and souls are composed by a symphony of thoughts and actions which are equal and can be compared to exactly. In recent years there have been studies that say that stress can cause a variety of ailments including, sickness disease and even cancer. Anger, hate, and envy have their own set of circumstances as well, especially if combined with action. A thought of hate, anger, and envy can just be a thought, but if you act upon these feelings karma will surely find its way into your life. Those particular feelings carry with them a very heavy negative energy, and I suggest that if you are confronted with such energies, do not feed into them, and let the energy be reflected by your positivity. If you buy into someone's, hate, anger and envy, by reacting to it equally, you have just become an active partner of that energy, and if you play with fire, the fire will burn you consequently.

Make today be the day that you decide to design your lifestyle in a way that will benefit your mind, body, and soul. Now is the time to begin the construction of who your heart and the almighty creator of the universe desire you to be.

∗

If you look outside yourself sometimes it is hard to find what the real meaning of life may define in your unique situation. Applying all your energy to find out what this meaning may be can sometimes seem very challenging, however, each day you may find new reasons and philosophies that change your everyday life. The average person, in fact, does not really even notice that they are in complete control of their own circumstances and reality, leaving most people feeling hopeless and at the mercy of their present reality.

In that situation, where you feel powerless, you pretty much are; you have installed that sense of feeling into your own soul, harboring that feeling each day, nurturing it until it grows to be a very real and dangerous emotion in your life.

To reverse the effects of self discontentment you must look inward and see what it is that you are really doing to yourself. You can either empower yourself or be disempowered by what is happening in your life right now. By exercising the key ingredient called faith; which means unhindered belief, if you use faith at a tool you can find that most of the things in your life from this point on, seem to get a little easier. Being in fear is a disease that's plaguing society at this very moment.

There is no magical anecdote that makes you different from anyone else, so it is your job to step away from the herd and become an individual. In doing so, your individuality will grow to amazing heights.

Positive energy will always defeat the negative and with a constant positive attitude you will be amazed at how fast your daily life will change for the better. We all know right from wrong, at least I would like to think so and to start off your positive lifestyle; you can begin by doing what is right. Honesty is a fantastic way to get started on your road to a better life. Honesty is probably one of the most important aspects in my life. It has gotten me in trouble, out of trouble, it has hurt others, and I have gotten hurt, but most importantly I have done the right thing. Honesty is a positive form of energy and no matter which way it is being used. Among all the events that resulted from my honesty, internally I held no regrets or guilty conscience in doing so. Those are very important things considering that we humans are emotional on a grand scale. A guilty conscience can be something that haunts you each day leaving you in a state of worry and despair and also making you feel bad deep inside.

One of the things we tend to do is look back at an experience that we regret. The energy contained it the experience stays with us and each time we think about it, it takes us right back to the same way we felt when it occurred. There are a lot of things that we do that we cannot change and still we hold the feeling of regret. It may also be the feeling of hate or resentment that you hold. Those feelings as well are not empowering you.

A way that you can achieve success in getting rid of those emotions is to put all your cards on the table; release what it is that keeps ailing you. This release can be the greatest and most meaningful experiences you can partake in as well as a very powerful tool in your growth as a spiritual being or whatever path you're on. By putting all your cards on the table, and what I mean by that is; we must show the world who we really are. Until we do, we are being dishonest with ourselves as well as others. Talking about this stuff with people, family, loved ones or even just writing it down can be a great way to express the things that you feel about certain ordeals. Buy a journal, composition book, or just a notepad, and try to write for at least five minutes a day, longer if you can, and if you can't think of anything to write, just write I can't think of anything to write. Just getting out what is on your mind is always a good way to release corralled energies and feelings that you may have cooped up in your mind and body.

The next great step ahead is to figure out what special gifts you have to show the world. You're probably thinking, I don't have any special gifts, but the fact is, everyone has a special talent or skill to show the world, it is your job to dig into yourself and find all that it is that you can do to achieve personal greatness and enhance the greatness of those that surround you.

Trying to decide what it is you want to do for a living or who you want to be can be a mind boggling task, or for that matter you may not be happy with what it is you are doing right now, hence, leaving you in a state of confusion and giving you the feeling of being unsure of your future.

These are all the things that most people think about on a daily basis. The way to minimize the abundance of this feeling is to let live unfold as it does. Universally you can only manipulate what happens right now and by honing in on a method to create the future it begins to be a step by step process rather than a hope and a wish type of situation.

By accepting the things as they come, the way they are, and realizing that everything happens for a reason, you can then start to figure out the big picture and how you have created the circumstances in the past. Have you ever complained about something and the thing you are complaining about seems to become this great big deal after you have focused on it for a short period of time? Of course, we all have. By doing so, you are putting so much energy towards it; it becomes this huge ordeal instead of a basic situation which could be handled easily. Focusing on solving the problem instead of focusing on the problem at hand can benefit you tenfold. Your problems will continue to get smaller and smaller until you get to the point that no problems can set you back; they are only an opportunity to grow. Step out of your comfort zone, get out of your box, and handle your problems large and small, what are you scared of.

A lot of people find it more comfortable to complain about things but for the most part, these people tend to become procrastinators as well. Complaining is an energy of a lower vibration, a negative energy that is only active if it is created, it is also an energy that is easy to get rid of if you put in the due diligence into doing so.

We can become our own worst enemy faster than anything else. It is crucial that we maintain a good focus on the here and the now because it is the only way we can stay in control of our life and our future. You cannot change the past but you can manipulate your future by what you do today. The further you are from who you want to become, the longer it will take. Unfortunately you cannot take a time out in this game. Life is a continuous collaboration of you and your efforts, how you put together this collaboration of effort is up to you.

Sometimes it is hard not to look back and visualize why you are the way you are, and can seem even harder to change what is already in place because of it as well. Intricately you must tie up your loose ends as well as letting go of the energies of the past that still remain plenty in your mind and soul. You are like a candle that can flicker at each passing breeze; it is your choice at how strong your fire burns inside, or you might let the passing winds diminish your fire. What do you want in life? Who do you want to be? Where do you want to go? Finding answers to these questions may help you find yourself and finding yourself is what you need to do to expand your soul. Only you hold the answers to these questions within, whatever they may be, you are the commanding officer in this scenario.

Some people like to blame as well. He did this that's why I'm like that. She said this, that's why this happened. Yes you can only take responsibility for your own actions, but there is no way that you can take responsibility for others actions. If you are constantly letting others get the best of you, you become the smaller person. Controlling the way you act without getting emotional about it can make the difference in every touchy event. Look at the big picture as if you do not exist in it; see how the people are acting, and see how most of what is going on is primarily based on the ego of the people involved. The ego just wants to be right. Honesty is the only way to solve this type of situation and if the people in this situation still don't agree, don't involve yourself.

Doing what is right will always be the way to stay on track. If you do not do what is right, you will be operating on a negative energy wavelength and you will be quickly consumed by the negativity. Consider doing the wrong thing as taking a couple steps back. If you want to consistently move forward, you must always do what is right. We all make mistakes but it doesn't mean that we cannot resolve what we have done. You will find yourself running in circles and not getting anywhere, this is a problem that the majority of societies of all walks find themselves in. A lot of people attend religious services on the weekend to redeem themselves for all the negative things they do during the week constantly keeping them in a level of mediocrity. This is not to say that everyone has this tendency but it is a very common occurrence in the world today.

Each day you should try to learn something about yourself or about the others. We often tend to think we know everything and in the battle with self we wind up not knowing anything. There are people who claim to know so much, but have not picked up a book since they were in school. I wonder where they get all their knowledge. There is a large distinction between street smarts and book smarts.

I was one of the people who thought that I knew everything but in fact I was only street smart, I had a bit of book smarts, but mostly on a mathematical and scientific standpoint. Until I decided to educate myself I had really only known the fundamentals of life, but didn't have complete control over my mind.

Education is big, whether you go to college or if you were forced to drop out of school because of a set of circumstances, it is not the end of your learning curve. So many people drop out of school and think that it's the end, so they start to do and sell drugs, go to prison, and just basically give up on everything. As long as you can speak, hear, or read, you can learn anything you desire whether you wish to do so at a school or on your own free time. The human species is the most versatile being on this planet. If you can dream it, you can achieve it no matter how big the dream. Do not limit yourself on what you can achieve; don't tell yourself you can't do anything, if you do, you can't. Make a habit of saying I can do that and by doing so you are putting a proactive energy out there that is second to none. You will find the answers; subconsciously your mind will find a way. Your mind is quite possibly the most amazing supercomputer that exists. You are the programmer of this so-called supercomputer; I would just suggest that you program it well. The way you program yourself is in complete harmony with the type of results you get. Each though is a seed, and if you continue to nourish that thought, if will mature. As everything in this world is potential energy, we are not any different than anything else we are all molded of matter and anti-matter. A thought is no different than a drip of water, the molecular structure of the objects may differ, but one thing remains the same, the two objects are potential energy. This potential energy can become either a negative or positive energy field, similar to that of a magnet or electricity which can contain a negative or positive charge. The entire universe is composed of elementary particles.

Our brains are like electrical power storms; they control every thought, movement, emotion, and control each and every bodily function. If we touch water, our mind delivers a message that says this object is wet, or if we touch something that is hot our mind tells us that the object is hot. In actuality what is occurring is a chemical reaction; the molecules in the objects are being deciphered into thoughts by our senses and our senses through cell memory in our brains are relating that to a commonality of feelings which in this case would be hot or wet. If we were never told how or what those particular sensations felt like our minds couldn't tell the difference.

This is why programming or re-programming your mind is a very important element in the advancement of your life. By reprogramming old methods into new ones, you can virtually change any aspect of your reality. If you say you can't change, then you can't; but if you say you can and you follow through with the actions following, there is an endless amount of growth you can achieve. In this process you will find the true meaning of your existence on this earth.

*

Each day we are confronted with a number of different choices that we must make decisions for. The circumstances for each decision we make differs due to the correctness of every choice we make. Finding the right choice might be difficult and sometimes we tend to make decisions based on emotional past experiences, we may also make decisions based on the thoughts and judgments of others. The fact is we can make a bad decision that at first may have seemed to be the right choice when it first crossed our mind.

Conceptualizing is always the best way to determine each choice that you make. When you do this you have to visualize the possible outcome or circumstances that might occur if you make that choice. There are many different possible circumstances to each choice. The best choices are always made when you are being honest to yourself and to others. If you happen to make any other choice, it will surely not flow consistently and in a normal pattern, therefore the results will not be consistent and normal. The determination of these factors is something only you can control at the given moment, and each moment varies in complexity.

We have all made disastrous decisions in our lifetimes and I am sure that there may be some regrets that are attached to those decisions. You shall not let these past decisions affect you anymore. The energy that is attached to you regrets will encompass any of your future choices and will assure the same type of results. Letting go of such regrets will allow you to move forward by giving yourself a level of self forgiveness. The act of self forgiveness lets you grow forward and even if you affected others with this decisions that you have made, your individual growth and forgiveness will be a positive energy that everyone will notice while in your company. One will say, "They have changed", and the circumstances of your new, positive, self-appreciating self will only get better in time.

It is very common that we make choices based on our emotions. These decisions are made in affiliation with a moment that occurred in the past. By making the same emotional decisions that we have always made, we do not have the ability to grow, hence having the same results we have always gotten. Most of our decisions are made due the amount of pleasure and pain that we may or may not feel during the choice making process. It may be the hardest thing to do when it comes to making a decision that will not necessarily benefit you. Most of us, from the time that we were children, have been trained to only make decisions that will benefit ourselves. Learning how to only make the right choices whether or not it benefits you or not, is how you must operate if you choose to grow as a human being. If you are able to be honest at all costs, the tendency of these painful decisions start to become very minimal and less likely to occur the more you become in tune with yourself, others, and things around you.

We begin to think as humans, that there are only two sides to everything. It is safe to say that every experience has a multitude of possibilities and there are not only good and bad, but layers and layers of different circumstances that are an equal reflection of what type of decision that you make.

Decisions, decisions, decisions. Decisions are what shape our reality each day and in every way. What to say, what to do, and how to do it are the questions that go through our heads hundreds if not thousands of times each day. What is the best road to take? Should I form a relationship with this or that person? These are also a couple of questions that if answered incorrectly by your actions, may affect your life in a big way. How do we know what is what, and who is who? That is something that only you have the answer to. Each person holds their own key to their destiny and also the path that they decide to take as well.

How do we control our thoughts? How do we change our reality? Stop asking yourself these questions and begin taking action in the self-transformation process. As I have said earlier, there is an energy attached to every word, action, thing that exists, and these energies are rated between good and bad, positive and negative, heavenly and not so heavenly, whatever scale benefits you the most. Each thought, action, and word you speak carries energy, even your facial expression, tone of voice, carry a wavelength of energy.

Conscious awareness is a set of words that describe the amount of comprehension that takes place in your mind at any given moment in the day. Conscious awareness is a fundamental element in the expansion of your soul, spirit, and mindset. Creating a control pattern that will be sufficient for your growth rate is all a matter of how fast you want to grow and how much commitment you want to put into it. Just like anything else you want to get good at you must practice as well as exercise and eventually it will become an activity as mundane as brushing your teeth or washing your hands. Your level of mastery in the subject of conscious awareness is in complete conjunction with the level of manifestation that you receive in your life, whether it is spiritual, mental, or physical attainment. While you are exercising your mind, what is actually taking place, is you are actually programming your mind like a computer. When you program a computer, you give it a set of commands that it must follow to achieve the desired result. In comparison to a computer when you program your mind, you are actually manipulating the neuropeptides in your brain to reconfigure the cells that make you think, or have made you think in any particular way in the present or past. By changing the molecular biology of your brain, you really are, in fact, reprogramming your mind chemically. This may all seem like rocket science to you right now, but it is really as simple as changing the way that you think about things. Positive thoughts will always be the most pure way to think. Without changing old thoughts that may have seemed normal before into thoughts that are more beneficial to everyone and not just yourself, you will begin to actualize all the things that before may have seemed impossible into your life.

Create guidelines to follow each day; know that each experience you go through each day and the way that you handle it, will be a direct link to the type of results you get, both large and small. Think of your future life as a tree, and the source of food for that tree being either water (good), or poison (bad). Now, think of every bad decision that you make as a dose of poison to your tree, inhibiting the growth and health of you tree. The only way that you can make sure that your tree is always growing is to always water it. The more you offset the growth or your tree with poison, the speed at which your tree grows will be at a much slower pace. If you consistently water your tree at a rate that allows your roots to absorb water, you will consistently grow and you will reap the fruits of such growth. Growing, and expanding your mind and soul, is a great way to find the proper path to walk on in your journey through life. Start using your mind as a tool to create, rather than a useless object that obstructs or impairs your ability to move forward in life. Commanding your life is the only way to command your life, and commanding your life is the only way to command your reality. Like a well oiled piece of machinery, you will operate so efficiently and so productively, you will become a source of goodness for everyone to enjoy and a mentor to the youth if choose to contribute to your community.

Part 3

The great thing about being a human being is the fact that we can mold and shape our lives at any given point of our lives, and that fact that we are so versatile allows us the opportunity to be who and what we want. The reconstruction of your life may be difficult depending on how far downhill you have fallen in the grand scheme of things. Above all, everything can be repaired on an individual basis. Although you cannot reconstruct the lives of others, being a trendsetter can always work by allowing your energy to possess the people around you. Energy is fluid and can fluctuate in and out of and flow in any direction. Possessing all the goodness is what your change should consist of.

Consistently apply yourself to anything that will help you acquire different levels of knowledge. Everything that you see, do, and learn, has a purpose on the grand scale of your reality, deciphering the images, sounds, and information that you come across is what allows you to change the way that you think and do as a human being.

Every day in your new existence shall be a day to learn, a day to see, hear and do what is in harmony with what you want in your life. When you realize that you have created a comfort zone for almost every aspect of your life, you will realize that you have actually been at a stagnant immobile state of living up until this point. Changing the way that you do things consists of only one thing, changing the way that you think. In a sense, you have programmed your mind to think in a certain way in all areas in your life and it is critical that you change these programmed methodologies and discover new methods as much as you can possible. You should even try driving home a different way each day, the more that you change your programmed way of thinking, it will become a fun and exhilarating experience each time you begin to step out of your comfort zone. Style your hair differently, get a new job, start exercising, move to a different neighborhood; these are a few small things that you can do to change your reality and the way that you have normally done the ordinary each day.

Just changing your immediate reality energetically, will transpire into all regions of your existence but you must always continue to grow outward or you will re-stagnate as you have before. There are always bits and pieces of knowledge and life experience that we can take with us each day and finding ways to grow, well, that is up to you. You pick and you choose the ways in which you want to change your reality.

Look forward and do not look back, it is very easy to find yourself dabbling in things that you used to do quite frequently if you hesitate to continue forward. Nobody is perfect and you will find yourself making small mistakes all the time and even daily. You should not hold to much weight on what it is that you would consider a mistake. Remember that nothing is a coincidence and everything happens for a reason, hence, you shall learn from what it is that you would call a mistake. Through all these so-called mistakes, you will learn and be one step further than you were before. If you let these things get to you, you kind of stop in place, similar to walking on a treadmill; you keep going, but you go nowhere.

This is often the status of who you were before, but without the know-how to grow past your basic instincts, you now possess the key to a new reality. You shape the key as well as what it is that you want to unlock in your lifetime. Some things are long-term and some things are short-term and you must always set a goal pattern that is realistic, a bag of money is not just going to fall on your head. Everything that you do to change requires effort and strength in your heart to make it past the struggles and failures that you will make.

As I have said before, nobody is perfect, so you cannot expect everything to happen perfectly. There are things that you must learn when you are going through the low points in your life; these are the tools that help you fabricate your future if you choose to use them as a source of strength instead of a weakness.

Decide today that you are not a victim of anything, it is your choice to consider yourself as a weak individual; you choose to be the victim and you choose to consider yourself to be weak. Complaining about what is going on in your life is a habit and can be a very bad characteristic to carry. Some people choose to complain about everything, and they wonder why that things don't turn out as they plan. If you cannot see the good in anything, you are not in tune with yourself, but rather a product of your outer world. Your inner world is a large part of what your outer world looks like. If you are continuously working on your inner world with goodness and appreciation of your outer surroundings no matter what they may seem, you learn to point out the good instead of the bad, thus changing your role from victim to a person who seeks goodness and finds goodness no matter the circumstances.

The way that you carry yourself i.e. hygiene, stature, health, is a direct reflection of how you feel on the inside about yourself. Your cleanliness, your bad habits, and your social circle, are also a direct reflection of your state of mind and feeling of self worth. If you look around and make a quick assessment of how you live, you will notice how your inner feelings have paid a huge contribution to what you have surrounded yourself with.

You may have been born into it and it may be a result of how you were raised, these circumstances to not attribute to your future and your future achievements. You may have been taught a certain set of values and morals that have not been completely beneficial to your life to this point but it does not mean that you are a victim. There are numerous amounts of people who have defeated the odds and great adversity; you as well can be a part of this group.

Realizing that the people that surround you, the environment that you live in, the friends that you associate with, and the circumstances that you have had, do not define who you are as a person or even define your future for that matter in the overall statement that you can make in life.

It may take a bit longer than anticipated to expand past what your present situation has dealt you, but there are a multitude of choices and possibilities that may present themselves if you choose to seek goodness rather that dwell into bad situations each day.

Commitment should be the rock that you stand on, with commitment you will always move forward. Commitment to finding the positive aspects in every situation, commitment to finding different ways to think, and commitment to strive for a new you each day. These are just a few different ways that you can commit. When you make the decision to commit, you cannot fall back, if you do, it will obviously set you back a few steps. The more set-backs that you have the longer it will take you to full accomplish what it is that you strive for. There will always be a few setbacks but it is our job to minimize them if possible.

The Continuation of your journey should be your number one task as well as what makes you push forward in the event of a slip up. Consider yourself as an addict of your past habits, and in order to put a stop to your addiction, you must change the way that you do things on a daily basis. Create new habits of thinking, your lifestyle, your health; these are all things that contribute to your advancement in the process as well as the tools you need to create a new foundation.

Make living a productive life your new source of purpose as well as your anchor in times of need. If life was a test, and in some regards it is, would you want to get a bad grade? Would you feel happy if you failed as a parent, a friend, a lover? How are you going get better grades? How are you going to change the way you have made decisions in the past? The answer is; you're going to try harder, and you aren't going to focus on what you did in the past. The only way that the past can help you is to show you better ways. You know what didn't work in the past, now you know what not to do in the present. Don't do things the way you have always done them. There is bits and pieces of things that you did do in the past that are what make you who you are, and I guarantee that they are not the bad things. I'm sure there is a list of great things that each one of you has imprinted into your heart. Take those pieces of yourself that you know, was or is still pure and magnify them until that is who you become again. There is no reason why you cannot become the vulnerable kind hearted individual that you have masked for so long. I guarantee people will enjoy your genuineness and open hearted gestures toward them.

There are so many things that you can do to change and there are so many different possibilities that are interconnected to each one of the decisions that you make. Try to make as many wise and honest decisions as you can on a daily basis and you shall transform at a much more rapid pace than those who do not or even those who do, but give half the effort.

You do not have to change, but inside us all, there are things that we want in our lives that would make us happy. When is the best time to decide to change? Why not right now? We sometimes feel as though we need a teammate when presented with the notion of change, we do not, it is nice to have a support group, but not always is your teammate going to want to stick it out with you. If there is one thing in the back of your mind that you want to have or do, but do not feel as though you can ever achieve that goal. Guess again, there is not one thing that you cannot attain, by changing your thoughts and the way that you use your consciousness, you may build a bridge to that dream that only seemed like an island for so long.

Have a chat with yourself, even out loud if you choose. Ask yourself "Who am I"? "What do I want"? "Where do I want to go"? "What kind of people do I want to meet"? Write your answers down. Hang up pictures of the things and the kind of people that you want to surround yourself with. This is what is called taking an active role in the visualization process. Having a vision of what you want can go very far, and having the images readily to see each day, tells your mind that, "This is what I am going to have".

Your reality will change at the pace at which you actively start to change your thoughts and actions. Action is what will build the bridge between you and your goals, without it, things will cease to change. Step into the unknown, feel what you have not felt. Go, where you have not gone. Be, who you want to be, and with these changes, the sky will be the limit.

What do you have to fear my friend? Fear is the downfall of society and what it has done for the human race has only hindered the growth of mankind. Fear has captured the dreams of entire nations, stopped the spread of peace, and had eaten away at us like a plague.

Anytime you are confronted with fear, have faith that all will be ok, and by breaking the chain of fear, you have broken the chain of hate, anger, spite, and envy.

Would you feel better if you let fear swallow your dreams and hopes? Count how many times you have been scared to make a decision, scared to act on something that required a timely response and you were left feeling regretful. These are those moments that will make or break the fear. What will you do next time you are faced with fear? Only you can answer that question and any other life questions that you may ask. Ask yourself these life questions on a regular basis, it will help keep you on your toes.

Each time you step up to your fears and act in spite of them, you are, indeed, in the hands of God. When you let faith and what you believe in, be your guide in life, you are in the right state of consciousness; you are at one with the universe.

Before you take on any endeavor, know beforehand, that you will succeed, and if you fail at what you are endearing, look again my friend. If you learn from what has presented itself to you as a failure, you have succeeded. You only truly fail, if you choose to avoid learning from the circumstances that have resulted from your so-called failure. As the master creator of our own reality, we control all the vocabulary and reactive information in our minds as to how we will respond to a certain event. Practice on changing how a disappointment makes you feel by insightfully using a different reaction. When you change your reaction, you change the way your mind processes these types of events.

Self-discipline is what you must be striving for throughout the process, some say that you must develop a habit, but if you don't truly feel in your heart that you want to do something, your habit will dissipate and you will relapse into what you have always done.

You must be self-disciplined in a means that lets you harbor what the true and correct way in dealing with a situation entails in your mind, and having done so, with complete faith in what you believe to be true, you will not succumb to the same instances that you had presently. Having said that, make a habit of making the right decisions, we all make mistakes, but you can build your understanding on how to deal with things by the accumulation of knowledge rather than tossing the towel in on your first sign of defeat.

If you have not exercised your mind in a long time, your brain might now be able to digest the information as quick as someone who has been consistent in the act of learning. To exercise your brain there are plenty of different things that can provide you with the mind power, such as; eating healthy foods, reading on the psychology of humans as well as self-help and motivational books, yoga, and many other forms of meditation.

You must believe that a healthy mind leads to a healthy lifestyle and healthy thoughts. Physical, mental, and spiritual health are all equally as important as one another, and you must take action by exercising all three as needed. You can't have one without the other so you have to focus on improving your life in multiple areas, equally and the same. Let your mind, spirit and body hold hands and walk in harmony from this point on.

Hold on to who you are as a person, there is always one thing that will always remain no matter how much you change; you cannot displace your heart. Your heart can be healed from strengthening your mind, so if it is your heart that has been damaged, then it is your heart that will be healed my friend.

Once you have decided to make the changes that you need to make, all you have to do is ask yourself "What do I want", and the universe will construct itself around you, and you're newly found way of thinking will be you're primary tool in creating your new reality.

*

In the grand scheme of your life there is an integral part of everything that you do and the way that the results may flourish. This crucial part is called faith, and the use of it had a great part in the abilities that you have as well as the outcome of every experience of your life. Without it, you cannot acquire most of the things that you would like to manifest in your lifetime. The firm belief, that you must have to achieve a common agreement within your heart and soul in order to complete the spectrum of a high sense of faith, is a set of guidelines and theories that only you can create. These metaphors that you create in your mind can surely be in consistency with the factors that are involved with your daily life and the events thereof. How you manifest your desires has a close relationship with the faith that you have. If you don't believe that you can have it, and you cannot have it. If you believe that you can have something with all of your heart, the possibilities are endless, and the opportunities of having and doing the things that you want to do will start to come to fruition at a fast pace.

First you must dispose of any possible past experiences that have led you to have those types of thoughts in your mind; you have created a barrier subconsciously that has kept you from excelling in the subject of material creation. You cannot formulate your desires if you have an abundance of pretenses that have aspired your recent way of thinking.

We all have these discipline patterns that are engrained in our subconscious, we have created them without the knowledge of doing so in the early stages in life as well as in the progression in time up to this point. This is to say that we have been the engineers of our awareness, subconsciously as well as consciously. We tend to create a safety net with our egos that keeps us from progressing past the extent of our belief system. Just like politics and religion, they are the deepest engrained belief systems. It's like trying to change a Catholic into a Christian, and a republican into a democrat.

To transform your underlying belief system you must thoroughly analyze any sort of belief that you are in total agreement or disagreement of. A large part of why we tend to think this way is because we all have a strong sense of opinions and judgments that concur with the actions we take as human beings, which is why we sometimes have the feeling that we are not in control of our life.

We also tend to have the black/white complex, in where it's either all good or all bad. We need to begin to look at things from both perspectives and start having balanced viewpoints on every aspect of life. Next time, catch yourself before making a judgment, try to make some good out of whatever you were going to misinterpret and find a happy medium. If few cases, you will find that everything is all good or all bad, the truth usually lies somewhere in between.

We have these belief systems usually because when we were children, we were at a heightened state of learning and a lot of the things that we learned, were actually passed down from one of our elders or family members down to us. To end a possible continuation of these, sort of family plagues, we shall change the way we construct our realities by breaking the pattern or cycle of judgment that our family has passed down to us carelessly. They were actually part of the cycle as well, but they did not have as much will power as you, and they were not aware of the effects that these judgments can have on their immediate family.

You can easily say, "My family is not like that", or, "My family doesn't judge", and the fact is that there is always a factor of dysfunctional-ism in every family, no matter how good or perfect they seem there is no such thing as a perfect person. It is by the understanding of one's true self that we begin to understand that of others, and in the process of understanding, it is then that we can see the light in everyone.

When you begin to believe that there is a bit of goodness in everything, you will begin to understand that everything has purpose and that through times of hardship, you will learn that these are all part of the constructs of faith, and only when you decide to thoroughly believe in something, which means taking the good from the bad and taking the bad from the good, you will find true faith.

Let your heart become softened by the sense of oneness with you, everyone and everything that exists in the universe. Put aside all your troubles and open your heart and mind with the thought that we all exist because others exist, we would not be here if it were not for others and what they have done in our part to continue the path of human existence.

Consider yourself as a life salesman, and with each bit of compassion, love, and kindness that you give unto others, you will receive a commission, a gift of compassion, love, and kindness in return for your efforts toward others. Think of everything that you do, say, and think unto others as something that you will receive in equal strength in due time.

As one looking in the mirror, you see your reflection, is it possible that what is radiated through the fifth dimension is actually a complete equal of what we do, say, and think; a reflection of time and space in our own reality? There is always what is mentioned as karma or the ethic of reciprocity, and many other ways to describe that what you do will come back to you in one form or another. Is it safe to say that we exist in our own reflection? Do our lives define what we feel? Are we an equal construct of our thoughts and actions? If this is so, do our prayers and beliefs manifest strictly because of how we feel within our hearts that what we want will materialize as the result of our faith? These questions have probably got you thinking on a much more complex scale than before, but the answers are still unclear as to if this analogy actually coexists with our true reality.

Belief and faith, the companions of manifestation, are the tools that must be used together to build the bridge to your dreams and your reality thereof. How a droplet of rain falls from the sky is not predetermined as to where the droplet will land, but it is actually the factors involved within the fall that configure its landing point. The wind, the temperature and the amount of moisture in the air are all contributing factors that determine where it will fall.

Consider yourself as a droplet of rain, but instead with a brain, a very powerful supercomputer that has the capabilities to define how the temperance's affect you path. The human species is composed of mostly water and has a gravitational magnetism with energy both universally and planetary, saying this, as a construct of my own theory, I believe that we are manipulative by the energies at hand in ar present reality.

In the field of astrology, the science of the stars, it is said that a person holds a certain energy which can encompass certain characteristics that are defined by the day, location, and exact time at which a person is born, most of these characteristics are a balance of which astrological signs that were present in the universe when they were born.

The magnetic energy that is created each day from the global position in comparison to the other planets, affect our internal compass and is what makes each day and each moment a new manifestation of internal and external energy, changing our present circumstances surely and in accordance with the way that we handle the changes in energy. This is why it is crucial that we retain a positive energy throughout our days, it is easier to detour the energy among us that does not quite benefit our superstructure as an individual.

So, what is faith? Faith is your ability to harness a positive focused outlook on the future ahead, knowing energetically, that the sequence of energy particles will collide composing what you have adequately focused on, and will in turn, create your reality. Of course there are no time restrictions on how short or long that the collective energy will compose the reality, but it is said, that a group of people focusing or praying for a certain subject matter, has miraculous outcome and the deliberation of such focus on energy, is what created the result.

So, is it all about mind power? Precisely! In the event that our mind goes aloof from the focus of positive energy, it quickly finds itself lost among our present situation. Life is inevitably a continuous learning experience, and in the process you may become someone who had let the world come down on you or the person who has made a mark on the world, the choice is yours, and the future is in your hands from each day forward.

How is it that others seem to have an easy and peaceful stress free existence? With the power of creative imagery in our minds, we sometimes build a story with an image and falsify what is actually true in the process, this being a natural habit of most individuals, prejudice is what is built by the exterior imagery of what one sees in an another individual.

How do we reverse this creative imagery and the results thereof? By focusing on positivity, a tool in creating faith and belief, build a good picture of no matter what it is that you look at creatively, and you will slowly detour the thoughts of negativity that flourish from these sets of judgments. Show yourself your own reality and creatively build an image of what you want to aspire to or create in your lifetime, the possibilities are endless.

To say that your attitude is part f your belief system is an adequate statement regarding the limitedness your mind has developed over the years. A bad attitude builds a bad existence, and a good attitude builds a good existence. We all know someone that has or has had a bad attitude, we have watched them grow or become smothered by the way that they perceive certain life experiences. Let them be the example of what can and will happen if you do not focus and believe in change.

Place your trust in faith and the power of belief, and you will have a magnificent increase of positivity in your daily life and the challenges that exist thereof. The universe will surround and work in correlation with your thoughts and actions, but only if used in unison and with true belief and faith. Practicing these techniques takes a lot of drive and both personal and conscious awareness. Is there something that you want and need in your life? Is there a place that you want to go? First you must believe that the results actually exist, then have faith, the rest is up to the universe to correspond to your energy that you put towards the direction of manifestation.

Part 4

Do you appreciate where you are in life? Are there questions that you ask yourself that question your current situation? Most likely, most of us will at least have a bit of questionable aspects of our lives. There is always a bit of work that we must do in the physical world that make us feel content with our present situations. Some of us are in wonderment as to why we tend to get the same type of results no matter what we try to do.

Why do we question our mere existence so frequently and why must we always strive for who or what it is that we imagine ourselves as being? How does this formulate how we understand ourselves as individuals?

Is there something that composes how we tend to manifest things besides faith and a sure sense of belief? I believe that how you value who and what you are now are a big factor on whom and what you will become in the future. How could you attain something that you do not quite feel comfortable with? How can you be, do and have something that you don't think that you deserve? Without gratitude you cannot empower yourself to achieve anything greater that what you have always gotten, and for a large part, meet the people that can help you get there. Gratitude is your attitude of thanks and how you appreciate the things and people that are in your life right now in your present situation.

Having the understanding of these elements in life and how they are interconnected, are the fundamentals that you must entertain in your mind to move forward. How can you have something better if you don't value what you have now?

No matter where you are right now, no matter if it's a relationship, an object, a place, if you are not grateful, you will not move past whatever it is that you are right now. The reason being is that when you tell the universe subconsciously, that you don't like where it is you are at today, you are blocking the circulation of energy and what you are actually doing is giving yourself more of what you don't want on many levels.

Why?

Because, when you have the state of discontentment in your mind, it is actually a barrier, shutting the circulation of energy flow, thus causing an immediate reflection of the same energy back to you, sort of like throwing a rubber ball at a block wall; it will bounce back at you.

Life is a mirror of who you are, what you see, what you think, as well as the perception of these and other things around you. The level of appreciation you give to each element of life defines how fast you may get to the next level, and so on, and so forth. From the smallest thing on forward, let yourself adjust the reception and the perception of how you feel about the basic things in life. Consider every element a godly creation full of importance and significant meaning. Accepting and acknowledging everything as a piece of the puzzle in our lives, a piece that fits perfectly into your personal existence.

Is there something that you are mad or agitated at? Has something made you feel more aware of your temperament? These outside factors will always be knocking on the door of your nerves. In the same effect as mentioned previously in this chapter, you have to realize that these things that ail your mind are actually supposed to be beneficial in your growth.

That sounds weird, but, if you think about the way that these things effect you on a daily basis, you would understand. The less that these things effect you, the more you can focus on the things that will actually benefit you. By using the power of gratitude, your perception of such things will tend to make a complete turnaround; you will now decide that every experience is to be valued and not an object of dismay. If you let things affect you, they will, and if you don't, they won't; a simple process that can only be mastered by practicing every day.

This element of re-programming your mind is one of the most powerful objects on the level atomical energy flow in the quantum physical realm. On the broader spectrum of things, you must tie into the universal energy that is abundant everywhere. Although you may not see or hear the energy that is around you, it's presence is far more potent than you may imagine, and to tie into this energy, you must get into sync with it.

There are many ways that you can get in touch with the energy around you, one of which may be a form of meditation, whether it is yoga, a breathing exercise or just taking a visit to a place in nature, all of which are different ways to connect with the energy that surrounds us all.

The energy source around us is so abundant, but fluctuates with our own internal energy synchronistically, so we must entertain this energy accordingly. To do this we must hone into the powerful energy within, and express it only on a positive level outwardly, remember you must also deflect the negative energy that exists around you as well. There will always be bits and pieces of negativity that surround you, energy that you must learn how to detour and finding a method of meditation with help you rebalance your state-of-mind accordingly.

This balance must be created within your mind on a spiritual level, whether the energy is good or the energy is bad, you have to balance it out; taking the good from the bad and the bad from the good so to speak. You always find more benefit in that form of mediation than trying to completely exclude the bad, remember, you must learn from each of these experiences, as well as be completely grateful for them, and use the knowledge you find to move forward in your life.

Having gratification is the most powerful element in the process of manifestation in your life, and must be one of the hardest to maintain as well. Creating a control pattern within your mind that allows you to realize that everything is just, is the single most important thing that you must entertain to make the process work. Knowing that everything is and will always be the way it is for a reason, is the way you have to look at things, and understanding that you may find good out of not do great circumstances in the first step.

The whole meaning of all this, is to enjoy your life, and what better way to do that, than being in contact with the universe on the level that, you know God has positioned the circumstances in your reality to make you learn a particular aspect of life that will strengthen you.

Beyond this, the ability to be thankful for everything that exists in your life right now is really the only thing that matters, it's the only way you can manipulate your universe accordingly, accompanied by a few other aspects of conscious awareness. Your desire and wherewithal are also the determining factors of how strong your consciousness will become. You're emotional habits as well as your opinions on many different subjects will have to sometimes be reversed to many degrees, this is the only way that you can make this work.

I've met a lot of people who artificially take on the job of a higher consciousness. They read the books, they do the meditation, but on a daily basis, they still utilize the same limiting beliefs and opinions in their minds. A complete self-brainwashing is the only way to go. That sounds kind of extreme, but in this segment of conscious awareness, you must set all of your limiting past beliefs free and begin understanding ones that will benefit you in a more proactive way.

A lot of the time, it seems to be the little things that get to us, and if you add up all the small things, they build their self into much larger things as the result of storing the energy that is attached to them. So when in fact these small issues seem to be very minimal, just the fact of letting something so small get to you, it just seems to occur more and more often until all the small things are built up into a compiled source of negative energy which affects you on a much larger scale.

More often than not, we fall victim to our own thoughts and emotions, not the thoughts and emotions of others. If you think of things on that context, you begin to see how your thought process truly affects you and your surroundings. You are, by default, the one who defines every circumstance in your life, and a large part of how you define your reality in most areas pertains to how your opinions and beliefs fluctuate on a regular basis.

How do you react to things? Do you find yourself focusing on the negative aspect of things rather than the good? Do you know what the word martyr means? There are a lot of people who have the tendency to magnify certain things that would not necessarily have that much weight, and turn them into something that affects them tremendously, causing them pain. On many different occasions, those same people may use this as an act, causing people to offer sympathy to them.

If those people can manipulate others to their benefit, how come they cannot manipulate themselves to benefit themselves? Where do people learn such behaviors? Most of these traits are mostly learned from family members and peers through adolescence and early childhood as the mind is developing.

This construct of information that has developed when we were young, has become a way of living each day, that is why it is so important that we are careful as to the behaviors that we possess while we are around children. When children are at that age, they are at a heightened state of growth, both physically and mentally, but it is often at that time that the child receives less attention.

It is evident, that at this age, we must teach the children the fundamentals of gratitude, faith, and belief as well as the affects of positivity and negativity in their lives. Be creative and come up with a fun way to do this, I assure you, that eventually, you will see a large difference if not becoming a way of life for your child. The closer to being a teenager the more difficult it will be, but everything is possible.

The earlier in life that you learn to focus on the positive, the easier it will be to maintain that energy as a child grows older. I have noticed that people don't really emphasize how important it is for a child to learn this at a young age. I think that many of the things that manifest from teaching them early, such as involving themselves with a better group of friends, not to mention smarter friends. Of course they will still encounter tough situations, just like anyone else, but they will have a heads up on taking the proper course of action.

Most people carry baggage that they have acquired when they were children along with them as they go through life, some of which try to block it out, or are completely unaware of how the things that happened when they were young are affecting them.

Do we have a choice as to what kinds of situations will occur in our lifetime? Somewhat, but more importantly, we do the ability to choose how these events affect us. What type of life would you live if you were grateful for all the things that have taken place in your life? Is there a certain chain of events that root from events that have happened earlier in your life? Absolutely, the way things tend to happen, are compilations of the way that you have thought in the past. If you continue to do things the same way, you will always get the same results, that is why it is important that you stay in tune with your ability to have a conscious awareness of the things that are happening around you, always being grateful for what life brings you, whether it's good or bad.

Each day, try to think of someone or something that you can appreciate and give thanks to; these are the beginning procedures that will put you on the path to being a grateful person in every aspect of your reality.

Think of a past event that you went through that may have been tough, or hard on your emotional and physical well-being, now think about how that event has prepared you for something that has happened recently. This time around, even though it may not have been completely similar, there are bits and pieces that have made the recent situation a lot easier to digest than the first time that the similar event occurred.

When do you begin this process, and how fast does it begin to make changes in your life?

The answer is: there are no time restraints.

The only time restraints that are given to such physical change in your life are the time restraints that you give yourself. We sometimes hold a sense of disbelief in these processes, and if you do not have true faith in what it is that you are trying to achieve, the process will not operate at the speed at which that you desire.

Digging deep inside is what is often necessary when trying to find the strength to get past the events that have affected you so heavily in your lifetime. Every day is a new day and you cannot expect to change the world in one day or perhaps your world for that matter. Some days you will accomplish much, having the feeling that you can take on the world, and some days you will feel as if the walls of life are closing in on you. All these different strengths and weaknesses are consistent with how your internal dialogue is being affected by the positions of the planets in our universe.

As the tide of the ocean is pushed and pulled gravitationally by the moon, our bodies are equally as resistant to the gravitational pull of the planets and the moon and earth. Like a triangulation of the planets and us we become an intermediary that feels the effects of the universal polarity. This happens because our bodies are composed of energy, a circulation and fluctuation of both positive and negative energy, and with that being said it is why our days, emotions, and thoughts are different each day. All these factors are taking place every day and the fact that we have no power over the position of the planets and the energy emitted, is why we must control our energy individually, adapting to the energies around us synchronistically and accordingly.

✳

Too often we find ourselves not doing what we want to on the basis of not having someone to do it with, and in the event, we tend to not do what it is that we want to do. Although it is always good to have a companion in the things that we do in our lives, it is also necessary that we become a self-sufficient individual, doing what we want to do rather than doing something just because someone has agreed to do something with you.

The unfortunate thing is that we as human beings are social creatures and tend to get caught up with what others are doing and we put a lot of focus and importance into the actions of others. As an outside viewer, it can sometimes be easier to focus on what others are doing; after all, they are who we are surrounding ourselves with.

We often become who we associate ourselves with as well. You have heard of, "Like attracts like", well on the grand scheme of things this statement is very true. If you look at the people that you surround yourself with, you will see a commonality between you and everyone that you normally associate with.

Are your friends and family holding you back?

Are their viewpoints holding you back from you making your own decisions?

In every social structure, there is often a lead individual that everyone wants to emulate. This person usually has the prime opinion in the particular social group.

Isn't it time that you look up to yourself as a force to be reckoned with?

All you need is a little confidence in yourself and the things that you want, and you will notice immediately how fast things will begin to happen your way. If you start to believe that your opinion matters and what you want to do is important to your soul and well-being, you will start to feel stress-free and light on your feet, accomplishing more and more, each day.

Once you learn how to depend on yourself and on your own points of view, it will become clear to you that there is more to life and the fact that you can now solve your own problems, your anxiety levels will decrease as you become more independent.

As a key to your existence, you should never really give up the associations with others as long as they do not suck you dry energetically.

Once you become more self-sufficient, you will notice that people will come to you for advice, almost frequently these people will seek your opinion for everything that they do not understand. Be careful as to who you give advice, it can become a very pain-staking thing if you have bushels of people that are seeking your advice. Sometimes it is best that these people need to figure out what it is that they are seeking on their own. You should never truly give them a path to follow, but rather give them an open-ended question, that requires them to find the answer.

Never tell anyone what to do, but instead, point them in the right direction by giving them a metaphorically speaking point of view, hence leaving their minds to ponder, how and what will get them to point B. If you give them all the answers, they will not learn anything. Consider life as a test, and if you give them all the answers, you are not truly giving them the ability to learn.

If you think about how a lot of your lack of self-adequacy had developed, you can reflect a lot of that upon your childhood and the way that you were raised. Many people allow themselves to do everything for a child.

In the early stages of child development, a child learns at a faster rate than we as adults do, and this is due to the fact that their brains and bodies are growing in unison. If we were to continue growing at the rate as we did when we where children, we would be giants.

So, if you think about how essential it is to give the child a sense of independence at an early age, they will become less dependent upon you when they get into their adolescence stages of growth. Having the ability to figure out things on your own is a very valuable trait to possess throughout life, and you could become an example to follow for your children and your children's children and so forth.

You can only gain independence by watching and listening to the things that happen around you and you should never hesitate to ask a question.

The only stupid question is the question that you do not ask. We have all heard, "Ask and you shall receive",

This phrase holds great truth and if you don't know the answers, I suggest that you ask.

Sometimes asking requires confidence.

"What if they think I'm stupid?"

"What if they don't know the answer, and I create a hassle for them?"

These, among many other questions, are the things that go through our heads sometimes when we get the feeling that we might want to ask someone a question.

Honestly, you must step out of your comfort zone, place one foot ahead of the other. The worst thing that could happen is that they don't know the answer, and if that happens, just ask someone else. If they don't know, find the answer, and the people who did not have the answer in the first place will be happy that you found the answer and you may even be praised for your efforts.

Imagine if you don't ask, you are putting the glory into someone else's hands. These and other small stepping stones can be the rung on the ladder that puts you ahead of the others and can mean the advancement of your career as well as many other situational endeavors. When you are at the mercy of all the elements in the world without the strength to do things on your own, you are left to blow in the wind, getting taken in whatever direction your reality.

The point of getting in touch with you individuality, for one thing, is to find who you really are as a person. When you put down all your guards (the fabric that holds you back), and truly find your vulnerabilities, you can finally exit the gates of your comfort zone. Until you analyze yourself and find all the undesirable, unbeneficial, qualities that you possess, you cannot find what it is that you need to work on. Until you can look at yourself honestly and say to yourself,

"This is what I need to work on", or

"I acknowledge my problems, and will work on repairing myself",

There are many ways that you can tell yourself what you need to do, but until you honestly come to terms with your ego, you cannot work on the underlying issues at hand. Everyone has an ego, and if you say you don't have one, that means you have an even bigger one than you than normal.

Your ego and your stubbornness have a great deal of weight when it comes to getting past those barriers that you have fabricated.

You may feel as though you have been running in place or for the most part not living the life that you have always dreamed of. You have to look at it like this; do you live other people's dreams or do you live your own? How can you truly flourish if you cannot blossom as an individual? Of course you cannot build a castle on your own, but why would someone want to work with you if you cannot carry your own weight? Without finding your own values, you can't be of any value to anyone else, it's sort of how you become a distinct individual in your social group, and it's how leaders become leaders.

By learning how to build your personal value, you begin to excel in all your personal endeavors so noticeably that you begin to use this in every part of your life.

I'm sure you know someone that insists that they are cool and use ignorant gestures and fashion themselves as large children and think that they are the next big thing. Ego itself is fueled by insecurity and the fruit that you harvest from these sets of feelings and actions can only be associated with loneliness and self-righteousness, neither being a productive way to live your life.

Although confidence and cockiness are very similar from plain sight, they are actually very different in definition.

Cockiness can be defined as: An overwhelming sense of self-righteousness to the point where one may think that they know everything and cannot do wrong.

Confidence on the other hand can be defined as: A humble approach to something that you aspire to, noting factual possibilities as possible circumstances in the process, but believing that the best probabilities will manifest.

There are also many variations of each and the heightened state of your ego, variably will determine how each one is defined. Cockiness can sometimes be molded into confidence by the perpetrator if they carefully manicure the needless negative energy that is accompanied by it.

If you already have a good relationship with confidence, you may still adjust the level of confidence by honing in on your level of appreciation for the diverse amount of possibilities and know that everything is, and will always, occur in proper sequence for a certain reason.

All these levels in between cockiness and confidence are a matter of how you choose your thoughts as well as your level of conscious awareness. How you manifest things in the physical world is dependent upon how proactive your thoughts are. When you have an agreement with the universe as to what you want and how to get there, the reactive nature of the positive energy is what helps you manifest the things that you want and ego would be what is considered as something that would hinder the outcome of your confidence.

How can you truly make a difference on the people around you if you do not have and characteristics other than that of a follower or a self righteous individual? Life is not a game in which you are out to deceive others with the purpose of enriching your own life but a rather a journey in which you help others with the intent of enriching their lives. Energy is reciprocal and if you help enrich others lives; as a result, your life will be enriched.

In the business world the chain of command is often set by the amount of challenge one can handle, so doesn't it make sense to stand out? When you excel past others with your high degree of effort, it is pertinent that you remain humble, because if you flaunt yourself around like your better than those who you have surpassed, the people in power will not praise you for your efforts and the chance of a promotion will become slim and your cockiness will deem you as a fool.

Back to the subject at hand, independence is not necessarily the statement of being alone or secluding yourself like some sort of nomad, but in the grand scheme of things it means that you're ambition and will for individual success is something that is noticed by the people around you. If your will for success is not strong, or you don't exactly have something that you aspire to do or see, then maybe it's time to get creative?

When you visualize happiness, what do you see? If it's having a great family life, or traveling the world, you first have to put your mind there before it can become a reality. If you cannot visualize happiness, then you may have to look back at the things that used to make you happy, and if that doesn't work, you may have to take your time and think of it a little longer.

Anything in the spectrum of life as you know it can be achieved, and without the want, the need will never follow, without your action the bridge will never be buil between you and your desires.

Closing the gap between now and where you want to be is honestly the difference between doing and not doing. Fear plays a role in your decision making process as well as what fabricates a barrier between taking the extra steps that are crucial in your evolution as an individual. How do you overcome the fear of making a decision? By making sure that you consider how you will feel if you do not make that decision.

Often, the pain that you feel from not making a decision will become larger than the original feeling of fear that you had when you chose not to make the decision. We truly are the only thing that stands between ourselves and our destiny.

I have heard people say that they are not after success or material possessions, and for the most part, are the same people that are constantly complaining about the things that they don't have. Just the simple thought of saying "I don't want success", or "I don't seek material possessions", actually puts the vibe out into the universe saying that you don't want money or things.

Success could mean the feeling of comfort or even just the sense of accomplishment. Why wouldn't you want to accomplish anything? On the same note material possessions could be defined as, food on the table or a private jet. Be careful what you say because the energy that you emit, is the energy that you receive.

Anticipation, joy, acceptance, fear, surprise, sadness, disgust, anger, optimism, love, submission, awe, disappointment, remorse, contempt, and aggression are extremely powerful emotions and when they used in accordance with your passion, you will reciprocate the same type of feelings and emotions towards yourself from others around you. Energy is contagious and every word carries source energy; hate carries a definite bad energy, even when you say the word hate it makes you get butterflies. The word action has a very forward, flowing energy. Even the word music holds energy. The point of all this is to convey the message that everything you do and say will be held against you, literally, so on a broader note, we all have plenty of work to do as individuals.

*

The universe is composed of energy, whether it's on an atomic level or on a grand scale, light years away. With the universe as well as the human body being composed of energy, it is evident that there is an absolute level of connectivity. Vaguely, you can say that like attracts like and similar strains of energy tend to attach themselves to one another. With a broader understanding of how we are actually connected, you will find that with each person that you meet, you can find at least one commonality, whether or not there is more than one similarity between the two of you, evidently you may not discover that unless you dig deeper.

Do you ever wonder why you are brought into contact with a person? Do you believe that there is a grand meaning for every interaction that takes place in your life? Unless you believe that every person that you come in immediate contact with is, with total certainty, an important part of your reality, you cannot digest the meaning of why they came in contact with you. You should always have an open ear for the possible connection that you may have with a person, this is one of the ways that you can expand your soul to a much higher level. With each interaction, if you stay focused, you will find amazing things that present themselves, some of which can be opportunity, relationships, networking; these are all possible outcomes when it comes to notating your connections with others. It could be like having a pot of gold in front of your face, and if you are not looking, you will not reap the benefits. When you begin using your conscious awareness, you will find a certain connection with every person you meet. If you are having a bad day, you are more likely to run into people that are having a bad day, and of course when you're having a good day, you will tend to meet people that are having a good day. This isn't always the case, but if your conscious awareness is active, you will see the difference of energy between you and the person that you are interacting with.

Like any other source of energy, it is stored then it is released at a given time. In the form on personal contact, the person that you are interacting with was connected to you by the thoughts and the energy that you were holding at a particular time. You only attract the energy that you possess and that is why it is very important that you retain a good positive energy.

How can you control the amount of connectivity that you possess in your immediate reality? From the inner sense of intuition and the amount of conscious awareness that you have, you can heighten your level of connectivity simply by tuning into the things around you. As you begin to understand how everything is interconnected, you will find how things link and how you can use these links as a form of leverage in controlling your existence.

Your intuition can be the single most effective tool to deciphering the diverse amount of complex signs that take place in every event. Think of everything as a sign, a sort of a guide as to where you go next on your life path. Some of these signs may be very easy to figure out where as others may take a while. You may have a set of signs that mean one thing, the longer it takes you to interpret the meaning, the longer it will take to move forward. You may only move forward at a pace that is comfortable with you.

Have you ever had an instant connection with someone? Most of us have had the instantaneous feeling that we have known or have met a person that we have not actually met.

As I have stated before, we are all composed of energy, and the fact of the matter is that our entire body is controlled by our brains which send out little impulses of energy that tell our body to move, cry, walk, sweat; outer expressions of what our minds tell us. Without the body, the soul/energy still exists and may occupy another living form.

I'm sure you have heard of the term, old soul, this term actually represents the form of an old spirit which has taken the physical form in a modern body. When we have the instantaneous feeling that we have known someone for a long time, and we have actually just met them in modern circumstances, it is actually very common that someone would run into a soul-energy/spirit that they have met in a different life, hence the phrase that someone might say that they "Must have known them from a past life".

These and other notions may seem difficult to grasp, but when you think of a body that has ceased to operate due to lack of brain function, the body is pronounced dead. Since our bodies are controlled by electric impulses, what happens to the electricity that the mind occupies when a body is pronounced dead? The soul energy leaves the body and is released into the universe, this energy is eternal and may occupy many forms and may actually enter a new body (baby), or even become lost (ghost) in the physical realm.

The potential energy of all objects in this world and the universe are immeasurable. Although most of this is theoretical and based on a diverse understanding of several different philosophies, to me, it is apparent that energy must circulate whether it is dispersed or if it is contained.

The ability to connect your internal energy with the potential energy of others is a matter being able to sync with it. To sync with the energy that surrounds you, you must submerse yourself in it. Without attention/action you remain separate from the external energies, which is why it is important to ignore possible negative energy sources. When you give attention to something it will expand energetically and dynamically to your situation whether good or bad.

Among all things, our connection with nature is the most extraordinary. The vitamins and minerals that we are composed of, the planet we live on is also made of, as well as other living organisms. When you are searching for peace within, it is fundamentally crucial to get out into nature and relax. The power of nature is the most abundant of all; it is the stepping stone to your individual self awareness and an anchor for your consciousness.

Since you now have a better understanding of how the energy in the universe can help you thrive, you can now commit to making conscious decisions as to who you will connect with. Every person that you associate with is a part of you, and what you see in others is what you see in yourself. If there is anyone that you know that is not beneficial to your individual energy, you must divide yourself from them. The more negative people that you surround yourself with, the more negative aspects of your own life you need to get into touch with.

When you get into touch with all the things that you may be holding in, you may release them, and once you have done so, you may now find it easier to connect with others. Develop a method of keeping focused as well as using selflessness, you may now plant the seeds of goodness upon all the people that you are in contact with. If you remain a selfish individual, how do you think people will think of you? Do you think that they will have positive things to say about you? Do you think these people will be on your side?

If you desire to help people, people will desire to help you, and positive feeling will reside within you as a result of it. Think of yourself as a life designer. What kind of people do you want to be around? What kind of life do you want to have? Where do you want to live? Connecting with the energy at all these levels of life stimuli is a matter of choice, concentration, hard-work and perseverance. When you fail, get up and try again, and when you fail again, get up and try again. Even if you fail hundreds of times, it only takes one success to get to where you want to be. Consider every time you fail a learning exercise, and if you take what it is that you are supposed to from each event of failure, you are actually taking what you need for success.

Nobody ever said that life was going to be easy and you often find with people that have achieved great success, an amount of failure that got them to that point.

You may also meet someone who has always had great success in everything that they have ever done, you may want to open your eyes and ears around such people and see what it is that they are doing. You will usually find that these people don't let little things get to them, if you sweat the small stuff how can you ever handle anything big? The bigger the problems that you can handle the further you can go in life. How often do you see people that complain in a top notch position? Never, this is just an example of how attitude can be the fulcrum to where you want to go and be.

Sometimes you have to live life like a champion in order to be a champion; you will seldom be the champion without the effort. Effort is your ability to put a level of energy towards the things that you aspire to, it is also the needed level of action needed in order to have continuity into the universal flow of energy; the creative force of manifestation.

Find a method of tuning into your passions and dreams, and you will find a happy place in your heart and mind; this is truly your route to connectivity, the road to an abundant life in all areas.

Test the laws of the universe with connectivity and watch how your life grows in many different ways as a result of it. Plug into the energy of new things and start living in new ways and have new ideals in your lifestyle.

You must pick up the pieces of your past if they have been the hindering element in your life momentum; these pieces of you are an archeological record of your past, a painting of the things that have ailed you. How can you furnish your new self if it is full of yesterdays mess?

In order to completely dissolve the impurities of your past, you must come to terms with it and be able to expose it all, and when you do, you will then be able to hack away all the weeds that exist in your mental filing cabinet. This process may be tough because sometimes we may be unaware of the things that ail our well being. Subconsciously there is a reason that you react the way you do to every circumstance, most of which is learned behavior that you happened to learn when you were a child.

Many of the things that we do to today we learned when we were children, today is the day that we shall try to unlearn these things and move forward. In a sense, you will be reconstructing your thought process, from how you do things, and to those which you associate with, all of which are a huge part of your expansion. Do you want to expand?

Part 5

Love, the strongest human emotion, can be one of the most complex of the emotions, and also the most damaging if you do not make yourself completely aware of it. Most of us have had our hearts broken in many ways in our lifetimes. Your heart is like the little motor in your chest that makes you operate, without it we cannot function properly, or for that matter, sustain life.

Even though our minds control our emotions, it almost seems as though the heart in our chest is in complete control of how we feel. When our heart skips a beat, it is usually due to an event that either speeds it up or slows it down and affects us in either a positive or negative manner. How can this organ be part of our emotional superstructure? If you consider the fact that if our heart stops and we lose oxygen to our brain, we will indefinitely perish as the result you may consider the fact of its importance.

Could our heart be what creates our driving energy as to what makes our nervous system function? Does our heart work like the alternator on an automobile? By medical studies, there are chemicals in our brains that determine the sequence of how our hearts beat as well as what determine the emotions that we feel in response to certain events.

Now that you know that it is truly your mind that creates the emotions that you have, via chemicals in your body i.e. epinephrine, adrenaline, etcetera, it is more apparent that we must learn how to control how we think about things and the way that they affect us in order to truly have a handle on life.

Your emotional status is a definition of how you let things affect you, some people are continuously angry, hateful, and dissatisfied with their lives, and they are always wondering why things are so bad. This is caused by not seeing the beauty within anything. If you focus on what is not right all the time, all the time things will not be right. If you focus on the good, you will find more good, your entire reality can transform by the simple transition of how you think about things.

If you have an idea of how life should be, live it, don't make it seem unattainable, your emotional definition of what you think you cannot have may overpower the feeling of having the things that you want, this is sometimes stemmed from being a child, subconsciously we learn the bad habits as well as the good habits of our parents.

In many ways, we become a reflection of who our parents are or used to be, and in the grand scheme of things we can always reverse the effects of what has been engrained into our minds. We may have had negative money associations, you may have heard "Money doesn't grow on trees", or "We can't afford that", or "Money is the root of all evil", these among many others are small things that we pick up as children, and unfortunately we tend to carry them with us without noticing.

When we learn these things as children, we grow up thinking negative things about money, and how can you have something that you have negative feeling towards? The fact is you can't! This is also true with someone that you may be attracted to, but if you tell yourself "They'll never like me", or "I'm not good looking enough". Who wants to be with someone that doesn't feel good about their self? All these are emotional barriers that we have created to protect ourselves from getting hurt, but if you look at it from the outside in, who are you really protecting? Nobody! You are actually holding yourself back from the thing that you really want. Why would you do that?

The majority of the emotions that we have are composed of learning experience that we had when we were young or at a time of great hurt. The thing is each experience is different and you cannot expect every event to turn out the same. If you use these past events as a method of strength and continue to make steps forward with an open mind, you are on the right path.

How do you use them as strengths? The answer is simple, ask yourself. You are the only person that holds these answers, and sometimes you can only find the answer if you ask yourself the question. When you ask yourself questions, your mind will automatically find the solution, sometimes it takes more than once, but if you do it enough the answers will pop up much faster. Like exercising makes your muscles stronger, your mind will become stronger the more you exercise it.

What we take action on in life is dependent up the amount of negative and positive emotions that we have, another way to describe it would be to suggest the each emotion is either tied to pleasure or pain. As humans, we tend to strive towards things that are pleasurable to us and in doing so, we often try to avoid anything that will bring us pain, which makes complete sense, but can also leave us blind to the variables that each experience may bring.

If you consider that with each bad thing that presents itself to you can have a positive effect on your life, and can not only teach you how to see the good, but by also not putting so much emphasis on certain aspects of your life that would normally cause you a great deal of grief, this is how you become a creator of your reality. If you choose to make a big deal out of small things, those small things will become large and may overwhelm you. You are only as weak as you say you are, and if you have the tendency to doubt yourself, it probably roots from when you where a child or an abusive relationship where someone told you that you can't do something, you apparently started to believe them subconsciously and it has affected you to this day.

Begin each day as if it were a blank sheet of paper, and on this piece of paper there are many different things that you can fill up the page with. In reality, how many of your days are exactly the same? None! There is no way possible that each day is exactly the same, and if you say that your days are the same, it's because you must continually tell yourself that they are, when in reality, you know that it is not possible.

With that type of mentality, you are hesitant to notice all the things that may benefit your days. By thinking that way, you are blocking out all types of new experiences that may present themselves. How do you begin to realize that there is an abundance of good things for everyone and not just a particular group of people? You can do this by opening your mind, and when I say this, I mean that you actually take everything the way it is without judgment, when you judge a situation at face value you already have a predetermined answer for each event that takes place in your life, yes, this is very limiting. To sustain this mindset, you must look at each situation as an open book. This applies to so many different aspects of your life as well as the power to overcome judgment. When you stop judging yourself you can stop judging others. The intensity of how judgmental you are is closely related to your ego and your personal insecurities. In able to curve your level of judgment, you must stop and decide how your judgment toward others is related to the way that you feel about yourself. When you make it part of your awareness, it is in the foreground and you will have a greater likelihood of creating a different reality, because the more that you judge, the less powerful you become in your social, personal, and environmental state. This will also cause you to have a harder time seeing the opportunities that pop up in front of you. Open-mindedness is crucial to your involvement in your own personal advancement. When you approach things with an open mind, you can better decide what things in life will benefit you.

You must have a degree of patience in your daily life, the people that surround you will not always be convinced that you have changed your mindset, and most importantly, it is all for your own personal advancement and not for the sake of others, and you may have to find a support group that emphasizes the same metaphors in order to keep the energy flowing in the right direction. When you let go of your past thoughts and actions, you also have to let go the people and places that are associated with it as well. You must determine who and what is benefitting your present situation if you want to truly find what in life. Once you have done so, you can now attract people with similar interests, pull the weeds and let the flowers grow among you while you yourself are growing.

In this process, you have to analyze the types of feelings and emotions that you are currently using in your daily life and find which ones that you must remove or work on in order to live at ease throughout the stages of growth. You cannot completely remove all your emotions and even if you could, I don't advise it, but when you can distinguish the difference between the good and the bad ones, you may then become in harmony with your reality and make better decisions. The question is, how much do you want to change, and are you strong enough to create an internal emotional balance? Everyone has the capability to do whatever it is that they want, we as humans have very minimal barriers as to what we can achieve.

When the mind is joyous, so is the soul. When the soul is in harmony, so is life. Untie your restraints and feel the freedom through every inch of your being. As a note of confidence; keep your eye on the objective, it is very easy to lose track, but with perseverance through the low times, you will forge a new path that suggests abundance in every circumstance. Using your desire and your faith as a driving force, the mind can achieve whatever possible but only if you truly believe that you can achieve what it is that you aspire to. Whatever you think about will manifest whether good or bad and you should deliberately focus on things that are true and pure in your daily life. When you make a decision to follow a path to a certain goal or passion, follow it with unwavering faith, determination and follow through. You will find many road blocks in your personal journey towards your passions and there will be many times in which you feel like there is no hope, but beyond what presents itself, you should always carry on toward what you believe in. If you do not truly believe what it is that you aspire to, you will fail over and over again until you finally believe in your heart and soul that the things that you want in your will manifest. Walk the walk, and talk the talk, don't live in regret for the things that you did not do, say yes to new things, yes to opportunity, it will manifest if you believe.

Play by play, each day is a new and exciting venture that you can mold in your own way, grow at your own pace, as well as destroy at your own will. Your emotional structure is a composition of your attitude as well as a reflection of the types of choices that you make. When you wake up each morning, ask yourself, "How am I going to create my day"? When you do this, your mind creates a vision of how you would imagine your day being, the only thing that you have to do is keep a positive attitude through every minute of the day and the rest will follow. Of course your day does not go exactly as planned every time, but when you keep an open mind and realize that you should learn from the not-so great moments of the day and use them as an actual lesson. Learn how to take the good from the bad every time and you will begin to stop acting emotional to daily events but more intelligently.

Having found this gift, a piece of every person, you will begin to realize that you are the master creator of your own reality and not at the mercy of the world at large, you will also find that you can make better decisions as a result. In a round-about way, the decisions, actions, and thoughts that you have are what control your emotional superstructure in addition to the way that you react to the so-called negative things that may happen throughout your day.

As long as you continue to push forward, keeping a positive overall standpoint, there is really no boundaries to what you can achieve. Everyone has heard only the strong survive, but when you think of living, do you think about struggle or do you think about being happy? Most of us will say happy, and when you think of it that way, to survive is to be happy, to truly feel at ease.

Do you ever feel like the walls are closing in on you? Most of us have in at least one point of our lives, if you choose to break those walls, you can do so with consistent effort and perseverance. Although emotions can be both good and bad, we must learn how to decipher which ones will either benefit us or cause us continual grief. When you can tell the difference between the two, then is when you can use your conscious awareness to manipulate your reality. The good emotions are the ones that cause you happiness, and the negative ones are the ones that cause your discomfort, it's as easy as that.

How do you erase the emotional scars that have been with you for most of your life? The answer is, you don't, what you can do instead of trying to erase them, is to try to create a system in your mind that helps you reverse the way that you feel, think of how these things have made you stronger and not how they have continually made you weak.

No matter what the cause of your emotional distress is, it is a part of your individual growth pattern and happened for a reason, you are the only person that can figure out what that reason is. Dig inside yourself every time that you come in contact with an emotion that ails you and figure out why this feeling exists and how you can relinquish power over it.

Believe it or not your circumstances are built upon your emotional superstructure, and the way that you handle each event that brings up emotional distress. Another way to offset your feelings is to put yourself in someone else's shoes, someone that has been through worse, suddenly your present situation doesn't seem to be so intense, and the answers seem to make themselves more evident.

The degree of focus on your emotional control is equal to the degree of composure that you keep through any given situation, you lose your composure, and you lose the power to stay bigger than the problem at hand. Sometimes you will be hanging on a thread, a small distance between letting your emotions control you, this is when the initial choice has to be made as to whether you lose your composure or maintain control over the situation.

Your entire emotional makeup is composed of how you retain your cool in various instances and this is the approach that you must take on your day to day life to be able to get to the next level of consciousness.

*

Beyond all forces of action, if there is not something behind it that makes it go, an engine per say, the driving force cannot push forward. When you say the word motivation, the first thing that stands out is motive, what will be the driving force behind your motivation? Some of us have an inner fire that makes us push hard at everything that we do, and some of us have had that fire extinguished by people that have told us that we "Can't do this", or "Can't have that", these gestures that were so innocently thrown at us have scarred our will to break from most of our comfort zones.

How do you rekindle the flame that has been lost for so many years? Yes, put gasoline on it and make your fire so intense that there can be nothing that can put out. Think of all the experiences that you have passed up because you didn't have the motivation or the feeling that you could actually do what it was that you could have done. Right now is the time to make sure that the fire within never goes out. Is it your inner flame, or is it someone else's? Right now is the time to be accountable for what you do or don't do. Close your eyes and visualize something that has happened in the past, think of how it made you feel, think of how things may have been different if you would have taken action. A lot of the time we think about what could have or what would have happened, and the fact is, everything happens for a reason. Think of it like this, now you can look back at ways that you shouldn't do things. Now you can honestly say to yourself, "Next time I will take action and make better choices". When you fail to take action, you stop the flow of energy, and when you stop the flow of energy, it's like a dam, but in this case you're damming up your potential restricting the amount of growth that you could attain.

Can you think of someone that has been a negative influence to your motivation? Can look back and see how motivated they were? Ninety-nine percent of the time, those are the people that have no motivation and what they were actually doing was trying to make you feel as weak as they were. Usually people will point out something that they don't like in others and what it really is-is something that they don't like about themselves. These people were too weak to face their own problems so they exerted the energy towards you, and now there is a bit of it that has affected you on a long-term basis.

The great thing about all this is now that you're aware of it, and you have made it something you are aware of, you can now compare this to many other events and see how they have affected you collectively. When you begin to look for the answers, you will find the answers. Most of think that life just happens to us, as a child there was little that we could do to control what was going on, but now that you are at the driver's seat, you can now make sure that you repair the past as well as make sure that the future of your children aren't affected by your past problems Someone has to stop the cycle, this can be you.

Has there ever been a time in your life that you felt like you needed to be pushed to do something but in reality you just needed a little bit of moral support? How come some of us are dependent upon the praise of others? It always makes us feel better when someone tells us what a good job that we've done and sometimes we actually seek praise but the thing is you shouldn't expect praise from anyone, but instead just try to the best that you can and whether you do good or not, at least you tried. As creatures of habit, humans can only get better the more that they do something. You will find that you will fail your way to success, the more that you persevere through the times where people didn't think that you could do something, the stronger that you get.

Motivation can also be hindered by procrastination, when you have the habit of continually putting things off, you will usually wait until it's an absolute necessity, and usually when that occurs there is a great deal of stress involved . Why would you wait till the last second when you know exactly how much stress it will cause you in the long run? Some of us are addicted to drama and complaining about things and we don't even know it, if you didn't procrastinate you wouldn't have to complain, and if you didn't complain there wouldn't be drama. Think about the energy of the word drama, it doesn't make you feel good just thinking about it, now think about the word complain, it doesn't make you feel all that great either, does it?

Having a better choice of vocabulary can also be a trigger to what type of actions that you take as well as the circumstances that you happen to manifest as well. Collectively, you have to be aware of not only what you do and say, but also the way that you react. You could be exclusively positive most of the time, but if you react negatively and use a vocabulary that is not very beneficial, the chances are that you will not have a good set of circumstances as the result of it.

A defensive attitude can be an emotion the stems from your environment or it could be something that could have been triggered from abuse and is mostly a protection mechanism. There are many different things that can stem from being defensive and most people don't even know that they are actually being defensive when they are. Subconsciously we are trying to protect ourselves and our emotional construct.

There are many barriers that may restrict our internal dialogue, the thing that tells us to be more active, these are the things that we must dissect in order to move forward in our ability to become a powerful conscious individual.

The ability to retain focus is determined by how good you are at not letting the external factors such as your environment, peers, and home life affect your internal harmony. When you are affected internally by the external factors, you will lose control, this is among one of the challenges that you will face on your way into personal enlightenment.

If you look into the past, can you see what has influenced your motivation more than anything else? For me it has been when someone said I couldn't do whatever it was, that's what ignited my inner fire. If you can reverse what has weakened you into strength, you can find an extreme amount of hidden personal power and really make a difference in your life at a very rapid pace. Honestly I can say that most of my strengths have come from my weaknesses, and I feel the weaker you are, the stronger that you can become.

You should look into your life's file cabinet and find all the weakness that you have, write them down, then in a separate column find a way to change the weakness into a power and how you can actually benefit from it. At least once a week, look at the list and thing about how you are making the changes and how you have benefitted from making the change; the benefits section you may want to fill out a few months later, mark down a date three month from now so you can fil out the benefits section.

Write down at least ten in this format:

	Old Weakness	New Strength	How it has benefitted you
1.			
2.			
3.			
4.			
5.			
6.			
7.			
8.			
9.			
10.			

Hopefully with this exercise you will begin to see things from a different perspective. If you cannot think of a way to make strength out of a weakness, you're going to have to try harder and believe it or not, you can turn any weakness in to strength no matter how you think of it. The weakness that you may have had before now can become strengths and when it comes to motivation, there are fewer things that stand between you and what it is that you want.

You should always be up for a challenge, you know what they say, "No guts, No Glory", and a lot of this rings true. The more that you challenge yourself the faster you will grow, if you don't try, you will never win. Action is always the most crucial element in any circumstance, actions do speak louder than words and I really don't understand how you could really accomplish anything by not taking action.

Motivation would be considered something that you can only achieve by instilling it in yourself, after all, who really does rule your life. Once you decide that your life is up to you, and that you are the builder of your reality, taking action may seem like a new thing, but you will surely find results both in the short-term and the long-term if you decide to step out of your comfort zone.

When you look at yourself do you see a powerful individual or do you see someone weak? If you tell yourself that you're weak, you are and of course if you tell yourself that you're strong, your strong, but you can only create strength by taking action and you can only take action if you have a full understanding of what is hindering your motivation. You are your own worst enemy as well as your own best friend, the way that you define yourself, is the way that you define the world. Finding hope despite your present circumstances could mean taking action on a certain thing.

If you are afraid of rejection or the possibilities that what you act upon might not happen the way you want it to, you will find that everything happens for a reason and the fact that things don't always happen your way is just a testimony upon learning through your failures. Although we all want to have success in everything that we do, it is crucial that we fail every once in a while, otherwise we will not learn the way that we should. When we learn from our mistakes, we don' make the same mistakes, but if you don't ever try, you remain exactly where you are and you will not grow.

Think of life as taking a hike on a meandering trail, there will be many twists, turns, ups and downs, you may even have to take a deep breath and relax a couple of times, there may be even someone who passes you up along the way. With little concern as to who passes you, you shall always move forward, and with each step think of progression, think of what lies ahead on your journey. Seldom should you look back, but when you do, think about all the mountains you have climbed.

Make sure that each step that you take is a step forward, every time you slip into reverse you will have to cover the same ground that you may have already passed. This is why some people feel like their lives seem to be repetitious, this is the result of thinking the same way and doing the same things, but if you look at it this way, if you do the same things in the same way, you will get the same results.

Motivation, a self derived force composed of heart, passion, and perseverance is and can only be attained through sheer determination and your ability to harness the factors that attribute to your motivational strength and personal power. These internal strengths are comprised of your internal compass striking forward, a growth pattern drawn by wherewithal and ability to stay focused on your objective. If you want to achieve the things that you desire, you will have to push forward at an extraordinary rate which will be built of many sacrifices upon the way.

With hard work comes great reward and with little sacrifice, comes little reward. You have to keep your eye on the prize or point B per say, the objective, and when you do, your level of determination will not be minimized in any way unless you lose your desire. Your desire to achieve is equal to the amount of success that you derive from your life, if you do not put energy towards the goals that you aspire to, your level of motivation will suffer as a result. Once you tell yourself that you are done growing, you will start to wither with the tides of life, but if you continue to learn and adapt to new situations your life will always be filled with abundance and prosperity.

How strong are you? How far will you go to reach happiness? Decide today that you can do what you want, and understand that you can achieve the level of happiness that you desire. "If you seek, you will find", "if you ask, you shall receive", "what you reap, you will sow"; these are terms that we have all heard and that some of us live by are the fundamentals of manifestation and the building blocks of our dreams. Though elementary by understanding, you cannot defy the rule of reciprocity, whatever you do unto the world the world will do unto you. Everything is energy and whatever you do and say has energy attached to it, whatever that energy is, will reflect back to you at the same level. If you hate people, people will hate you. If you are jealous and unkind to people, people will be jealous and unkind unto you.

Like I said, everyone has heard of such a process, how come most of us don't live by this concept? I believe that some people have a lack of faith or even sometimes a lack of accountability, always blaming others and looking at others to solve their problems by pointing the finger. It is more honorable to be honest than it is to sugar coat a certain subject, the truth will always be the right way to handle any situation. The more you lie to others, the more others will lie to you. This is a perfect example of the law of attraction. Your level of self awareness will grow at the same pace you do as a person, and the question is, "How much do you want to grow"?

Your motivation will get much stronger the more you believe in yourself, consider yourself as a building being renovated from the ground up, first you will have to rebuild the foundation, then you will have to make sure the structure itself is sturdy, and when that is done you will paint this structure whatever color you want, following that, you will choose what you want to furnish the interior with. It doesn't matter how bad your structure was in the past or is right now, you can always rebuild the structure from the ground up. In some cases, there will not be any of the previous structure that you wish to hang on to and you will have to start all over from scratch, how do you want to build yourself, what will you furnish the interior with this time?

How do you rid of the elements that you were composed of in the past? It's almost as if you are recycling the good, and getting rid of the bad. No matter how bad things are or were, there are always bits and pieces of goodness that must be kept, your character is the true ingredients of which you are as an individual and must refurbished if damaged beyond recognition. As human beings, we are the most resilient animal on the face of the earth, having the composition of an earthly being and the spiritual makeup of a god, we are tuned to become the best that we can be, this is why we all have an unlimited amount of pure potential. Our ability to adapt in accordance with our ability to learn make us truly unstoppable and the possibilities of who you may become are endless.

Part 6

Truly and deeply, we are all seeking our own inner peace. With a feeling of peace and dignity, we all feel as though are lives will be better. How do we find this sense of inner peace? To many, we think that financial success or finding that special person will bring us to that level of personal serenity. Many of us feel as though without a certain material of physical object we cannot obtain this level of individual happiness. Although we would all like for things in our personal reality to be a certain way, it is mostly the makings of your inner self that actually reflect the type of material objects that we manifest in our realities.

This is the problem, we look at others who seem to be happy and compare our own existence to theirs. They may have what looks to be an amazing life; the smile on their face, the family that they may have etcetera. The happiness that is obtained within these individuals is actually a reflection of how these people feel on the inside. The question is "How do I become at peace within"?

The construct of our inner being is a made up of our emotions and the way that we feel about ourselves. If you have had a problem with your self-esteem or the way that you look at yourself as an individual, most likely you have suffered in the physical world as a result. Body language, attitude, and many other things even your ego are an expression of how you feel inside. Although we may consider these things to be a protection mechanism, they are actually the biggest things that are holding us back from getting to a higher level of inner peace. We often think that what we have in the physical realm will change the way that we think about ourselves internally or we think that the way people treat us can change us internally as well. When you decide to stop trying to please everyone and start trying to please yourself, you will not really see any results externally.

You might ask yourself, "How am I going to change my life if things are the way they are"?

Your outer world is a perfect reflection of your inner world, so you have to become a source of positive energy internally no matter what your external reality may be. If you look outward and see how your reality is very similar to your internal makeup you can see how the slightest changes internally can make a huge difference on the outside. For instance, the smallest things that you may not have noticed, such as the tidiness of your bedroom, may be the result of your emotional status of where you are living. In the event that you clean up your living space, your mind will feel at ease while being at home.

There are many different things that may not have been aware to you, even how you take care of your car. If your car is a mess on the inside and on the outside, and the fact that your vehicle may be your main source of movement from point A to point B, the fact that a car may be theoretically defined as movement in the physical world, it may say that your internal and external composition are out of order and that your placement may not be orderly on a physical standpoint. Let's say your car is immaculately clean on the outside, but on the inside your trunk is filled with junk and the interior is unclean as well, this may be symbolic of how you are in your life; you may be very pleasing to look at but your interior, such as your emotional structure is a wreck. This example may also be in comparison to how you keep your desk and many other instances in your life.

Your serenity is dependent upon how well you feel on the inside, how bad do you want to make a difference in your life is equal to how hard you try to clean up these minor things that may give you distress on a daily basis. You must consider this as an exercise for you and a loved one but what it boils down to; you must work on your individual reality.

Take a long walk, go into nature, find peace within and you will be able to dial into the small things that may exist. You may have never even open to this sort of notion, but from this point on, you will begin to see a multitude of environmental imagery that is equal to your internal mental distress.

Unfortunately, you cannot change anyone but yourself, you may be able to open one's mind to a certain philosophy on the conduct of their lives but in the long run you must decide to retain a complete focus of yourself. By doing this, your changes will be more apparent to the people that surround you, setting an example for them to follow, but only if it has been an obvious change.

Leading by example, and following your own path of personal advancement can be a contagious energy for your peers. You will often find that people will mock your obvious change, but life is not a game where others can control your reality, you can only create your own reality and the lack of acceptance of people within your personal reality can only hinder your advancement if you let it. It's a statement of how strong you are as an individual as well as have hard you can push through. People will call you fake, they will say that you are not being yourself, but fact is you have made the decision to become a beacon for your own individual power source.

We all have an unlimited amount of energy that we can diffuse in any way that we wish. The process in which you use this abundant energy flow can be used in both a positive or negative way, the choice is up to you. Negative feelings and emotions can only lead to a collection of negative results and circumstances. Positive feelings and emotions can only lead to positive results and circumstances. Both positive and negative, you are the one who composes the definitions of your active emotional structure.

If you cannot find a place to harness all the positive energy that you have within, you can close your eyes and visualize, this can one of the most powerful exercises in your personal enlightenment if there are not any immediate places to go within your community. By going within to find your inner peace you will get used to asking yourself for the answers. In the universal space of your mind you can find and visualize any answer that you may be looking for.

Learning how to keep your calm in what would be considered a dramatic situation is ideal when it comes to learning how to live in a serene state of mind. Each and every person can find this inner peace and some of us may have to develop a special way that we can reach this place. Deep concentration and a strong sense of faith and belief are the fundamental elements of knowing that everything will be alright when things get hectic, ideally you will become more virtuous as the result of your ability to hone in on your calmness. From this exercise you will become strong and unaffected by what would normally cause someone anxiety and stress.

Believe today that you can start making a change in the way that you feel and react to certain situations, don't wait till tomorrow or the next day, there is only one perfect time to make these changes, and it is now. How hard can it be to want to live your life the way you want to? It is as easy as you make it and the longer that you wait, the longer it will take to get to the point that you want. Your mental state of mind is equal to your reality; the way that you define things, the way you react, and the way that your attitude fluctuates thereof, are a gigantic part of how your life story plays out.

Your mental health can be the starting point of your own personal challenge. Your mental health can start to change by making some adjustments in your diet; eating healthier foods can provide more nutrients that your mind requires to operate at a better level. Vitamins and exercise can also make a difference in how fast that these changes can occur. You have to realize that in order to change your life, it is crucial that your physical, mental, and social health must all be equals. You cannot have one without the other and it really doesn't make sense how one could outweigh the other if you were to be completely enlightened individually. Saying this, you must design a way that allows you to focus on multiple aspects of your reality, in other words, you will have to keep mind's eye on all your different characteristics and decide which ones that do not benefit a good mental, physical, and social standpoint on life.

When you are in doubt, live without; the grand scheme of life is based on risk and reward, you must pay the price to obtain what it is that you aspire to, and the greater the sacrifice the greater the reward. After long exhausting efforts at working toward your dreams, sometimes you will feel as though nothing will manifest, you will feel as though you are never going to receive what it is that you want. Sometimes you may be inches from your dreams, this is often when one will give up the fight, end the hard work, and toss in the towel. If you would only give it a little more effort, a little more fight to the end type mentality, maybe you will reach what it is that you desire? How hard are you willing to fight for your passions and dreams?

Perseverance and the ability to keep your cool through those day when you think that you have made the wrong step forward, is so important; be a superhero, be impenetrable, become tough as nails, but only in a way that your inner peace and level of calmness is apparent by those who surround you. A kind, gentle, and serene individual is the one who holds strength, the one who manifests their desires.

*

In the quest for a happy life, sometimes we feel out of control, and adrift in the ocean of circumstance. The knowledge that we receive in our days either benefits of minimized the amount of happiness that we can achieve. Most of us were taugh or mentored by our mothers and fathers and family members and took on many of the characteristics that they had in our quest to find ourselves. Some of the information that we received, we have taken so serious that our ability to grow has been blocked by a wall of our own consciousness. Inevitably we must learn from our mistakes and find what it is that has been damaging our ability to flourish as an individual. Awareness is the key to finding one's self and the ability to discover a method of healing the wounds of the past is the answer or as insight as to taking the right path in a forward direction.

As humans we sometimes become cynical to the point where our sense of belief and faith become scrutinized, most of which is created by life experience itself. If your faith has been hindered by circumstance, how has it affected your well-being? How has it affected your attitude on life? Are you accountable for the set of circumstances that you have gotten in the past or do you blame others for the events that have taken place in your life? Why must someone always be to blame? If you were to take responsibility for the events and actions in your life how do you think that you would live as a result? If you could find a way to forgive others as well as yourself, the amount of stress that is fabricated in certain events could be very minimal. When one has forgiven others, one can forgive one's self and when you live a life full of positivity, your state of mind will be a serene environment and the disposition of your emotional construct will be forwardly enlightened.

Why do we become lazy when it comes to building a lifestyle that we can enjoy? What happened and how did we become controlled by our society? For many and many years, governments and leaders all over the world, have created a control system that forces us to believe that we are powerless and must follow the crowd per say. Why do we feel like we have to follow the crowd? As a human, w are a social being and subconsciously we develop the tendency to aspire and look to others for the answers or a path that has already been traveled. We often become lost on our voyage while trying to emulate what others have done and fee hopeless and powerless as a result.

We can only carve our own path and the fact that we want to take the path that someone else has carved makes it difficult for us to find good results because we can only follow our own path. If we would only focus on ourselves and not others we can find the internal set of life tools that have been given to all of us and use them to form our dreams and passions. The problem is that most of us seek the answers from the people that we trust instead of trusting our own instinct. It is always a good thing to educate yourself on the subjects that you are interested in, and the building of knowledge is something that you must do to advance yourself as an individual. If you want to know more about people, get a book about people if you want to know about money, get a book about money. You can find a book to learn just about anything. Consider each day a learning experience in which yo can add to your mental filing cabinet, expanding your mind each day.

Some only choose to learn about a couple of different subjects then seem as though they don't know anything later in life, I would suggest that you diversify your knowledge and take a little from everything, you never know when you will need the information. Information is presented to you not by accident, but as a sign, and if you decide to learn, the reoccurrence of certain events will cease. We live in a flowing universe of energy and matter, use your intuition to take what the universe is giving you and mold and shape your reality with the tools that are given. You must first believe that you can change your reality, it will not change in a week, but it is a life process and the better your energy, the better your life.

Collectively, you will see differences in your character, and the amount of knowledge that you obtain you will take with you on a daily basis. Consider the knowledge that you possess, tools to climb the mountain of life, how can you climb such high mountains without the right equipment? If you are poorly equipped, your journey will not be a smooth one. When you decide to change, your life will change and the universe will change accordingly to what you are ready for. Take each day for a test, a learning experience, a piece of the puzzle of life.

How much can you handle? How far do you want to go in life? Each day will bring you a new set of circumstances that either lead you toward your destiny or away from it, and when you choose to make the wrong choice, of course you are not operating on the right frequency, you must decide to operate at 120% in a forward manner and to do this you must have a conscious awareness as to the things you think, the people that you associate with, the food you eat and I'm sure you can find a couple of things that you need to work on that would help you operate at a higher frequency.

When energy has the ability to circulate, this is when you start to see results. Life is a river and you will either sink to the bottom like a rock, or you will follow the current like a well engineered watercraft. Even if you are being carried by the current you can still spring and sink to the bottom. Sometimes you have to steer away from things that will set you back, and believe me, there will be many obstacles in your path. No matter who you are, or where you come from, you will still have your own set of challenging events that occur throughout your lifetime. Determination and inner strength are the glue that holds you together through those times, and you decide whether or not the glue will hold you together. As individuals, we are all searching for something whether we know it or not, and the key is to acknowledge what it is that you aspire to. Become sensitive to your surroundings and how they can positively and negatively affect your reality. Let's say you are driving to work and you normally have to commute through a bad neighborhood or area in town, this area makes you feel anxiety and you try to quickly get through daily without spending too much time in it. Think of how you could travel through a different area that makes you feel more at ease, after all you don't need to feel like that. Its small things like that that make a huge difference in your well being and the more that you become conscious of the little things, larger things will begin to change as well. If there is a person that you have to deal with each day that doesn't have a good attitude or maybe they cause a lot of drama, think of how your day would be if you decided that you would not associate with this person unless it was on a need-to basis, how would this change your day?

Harboring things in your life that you don't necessarily need can cause a recirculation of energy that is attached to it. Pack-rats have all this stuff from the past, they claim that there is significance to these objects, but they clutter their life Imagine all the energy from the past that is connected to each one of these objects, how can all these things promote a greater consciousness? Fact is they cannot. If you want to clear your mind of clutter, you must free your life of clutter. The longer that you hang-on to the objects of the past, the longer the past affects you.

I'm not saying that you dispose of everything, there are certain family heirlooms that you just cannot rid of, but you must certainly free your immediate surroundings of objects that may harbor energy from the past. Look on the walls, the bookshelves, your closets, consider all these locations to be segments of the mind, each day you are affected by the images that you see and the energy that is attached to it. Now that you have a visual and a set of examples, now you know just what you need to get rid of, or get out of your immediate surroundings. You can put these things in storage if you insist that you need them, but then again, one day you will find yourself reminiscing again, bringing back the memories of the past. As a forward thinker, you don't need to facilitate past memories in your daily life, you either learn from the past or you don't, and there is no real reason to bring back the reasons why you either learned or did not learn what it was that occurred in your past.

Ok, here on the next page will be an exercise that will allow you to write down the things that you have been hanging onto, what they represent, and what you can learn from getting rid of these objects i.e. present from an ex-girlfriend/boyfriend etcetera, hat that you wore on the day of a family member's death. If you can't find anything, look again, believe it or not, there has to be at least one thing, even if you have to get rid of a person. If you really cannot find one, skip this exercise and continue reading the material that follows the next page, you apparently have done your homework. If you have decided that this exercise is not for you, please keep this concept fresh in your mind, if you do, you will find something that you may not have noticed before, something that may have been staring at you in your face?

	OBJECT IN YOUR REALITY	ENERGY/EMOTION ATTACHED TO THE OBJECT?	HOW GETTING RID OF THE OBJECT CAN HELP YOU
1)			
2)			
3)			
4)			
5)			
6)			
7)			
8)			
9)			
10)			

Through this exercise you have written down things in your immediate surroundings that have affected you on a daily basis without noticing. Now that you have made these things aware to yourself, you can now reflect on each individual object and how it has affected you and how it may affect you positively by getting rid of it. Don't feel as though you are being forced to get rid of things that you need, unless you feel that you need to go on each day feeling the same way that you did in the past. Consider this part of the cleansing process, a crucial part of your growth. When you wash away the stains of the past, you can now clothe yourself with new, beneficial, feelings and emotions.

Opening your consciousness is like opening your mind, when you have a preconceived definition for everyone and everything how can you truly expand into a greater consciousness? Live every moment for what it is and realize that every experience is different and that you should have your eyes and ears open to what you cannot hear and see, when you believe what others cannot believe, and do what others will not do, this is when you have reached the highway in life. Even though you may get caught up in traffic on the highway of life, with an open mind, you will be able to overcome any obstacle in your path.

Part 7

Communication, whether done via body language, verbally, or energetically, is an important aspect in everyone's life, how can you get your point across or convey a message without communication? A large percentage of the population has the tendency to hold back on communication due to predetermined emotional factors that stem from past events. With a strong sense of communication, you could master your life; communication is the conveyance of your feelings and emotions. How can you get your point across to the people you want to without proper communication? The answer is: you can't. Consider yourself in a different country where you don't know the language, you are left with the only option of following body movement in order to define what message someone is trying to convey to you.

Communication on many levels means that you must master several types of communication styles considering we do not all communicate alike. Some of us tend to be more visual, where as some tend to be more verbal and to some degree even hand gestures can even be an effective method of communication. I feel as though you must learn how to use each method effectively in order to become a master at communication. Although there is always room to grow in the area of communication, I use the term master very lightly, each day we should try to learn different and new ways to communicate. One of the strong points in communication is the ability to listen. When you listen, you are more inclined to have a better more accurate response to those who are trying to communicate with you. Having open ears, I found to be one of the most effective ways of communicating. Although when you listen, you are not formally communicating, but rather collecting the information that you hear, and after all, the majority of people tend to want to be heard rather that listen to someone speak.

By allowing someone to completely communicate what they want to say without interruption, you can analyze what it is that they are trying to communicate and have a valid and complete understanding of what it is that they are trying to say. Learning how to have effective communication skills starts here and follows with a more advanced methodology of response and action. Yes, this all seems elementary, but sometimes we must refer to the basics at sometimes. We often feel as though we must reengineer the wheel while going through life and we can sometimes fall astray, at these times we must go back to the basics.

Eye contact, facial expression, and body motion are effective ways of showing whoever is communicating with you, that you are truly listening, and honestly, how could you be possibly communicate effectively if you don't express your ability to have an open ear. In the event that you properly listen to what someone is communicating, you begin the transference of energy and when this occurs your souls collide, you are then harmoniously communicating with someone. At this level of communication you can achieve the results that will allow you to manifest what it is that you want in this world.

We often feel as though we can do everything ourselves. Although becoming self-sufficient is a great characteristic, we must realize that without others, worldly accomplishments can be very hard to achieve. Even if you don't necessarily want to have accomplishments to that degree, your own level of achievement can be considered a worldly achievement, this means that you create your own reality and in fact your own world, so worldly achievement refers to the manifestation of what it is that you are really aspiring to be.

With communication, you can repair, destroy, or create any type of relationship that you want, and with a good understanding in the field of communication, there are multiple variables and an endless amount of opportunities that can result from good communication. Why must one shut themselves off from the world, have they been hurt, why do we toughen ourselves to the world? We have created our own personal dilemma from the thoughts and feelings of others. Our temperance, our ability to cope on a daily basis has been marred. As a social species the human animal without spiritual instinct, commands itself by manipulation, self righteousness and abuse, it makes one's self feel bigger at the expense of others. Why have we become a self destructive being? The answer is to become closer to our soul, the energy that fuels the fire inside of us, and become more open, less, judgmental, and sensitive to the feelings and energy that we portray towards others. If all we are is energy, and the energy that is emitted from us reciprocates back to our personal reality, why would we want to do and say bad things, and belittle others when in fact the same energy will be reflected back to us? Subconsciously most are not aware of the phenomena mostly due to a religious context, but it is evident in many cultures that the same philosophy on energy circulation is almost standard. Why do we tend to judge rather than open our hearts to new people and ideas?

In a fear based society, we are told what we should and shouldn't do things and the aftermath of such outer control factors is that we lose control of ourselves and follow the acts and judgments of others. What happened to individuality and the manifestation of our dreams? Is this what society has planned for our existence? Have we become robots, operating to the chime of our leaders? Who is your leader? Are you in control of your life? Who is?

Today can only be what you want it to be if you decide that you want to control the outcome of your life without being jaded by the misappropriated control efforts of those surrounding us. Every day, we have built up this doubt inside that we cannot do the things that we want. We have decided that there are too many barriers between who we really are, so we just follow the herd and blend in with society.

In the same regard, we all want to be different, so why are we so much alike? When you put forth energy in creating a different course of action, the universe will supply all the pieces of the puzzle that you cannot fathom, you just have to make the first step in doing so. You know exactly what you want to do you just have to find out what is has been restricting you? Your first line of thought will be that someone else has been what has been holding you back, and you may be right but why would you let someone hold you back? Aren't those people holding themselves back as well? This is a perfect example of how we let those who surround us effect our inner control mechanism. Are you going to stop the cycle?

Are you going to pull your head out of the sand and get your legs out of the concrete blocks that you have fashioned to your feet? In order to move forward as a spiritual being, we must do so, how about now? The restraints that we put on ourselves are far greater than anyone else could put on us and this has to the sole focus besides keeping your energy flowing in a positive direction. As long as you maintain the positivity and keep a stronghold on your conscious awareness, you are definitely keeping the ball rolling.

Once you have reprogrammed your mental state to a point where you can admit that you are indeed in control of your destiny, you can now take steps forward in the right direction. You have to let go of what has happened in the past, forgive yourself and others if need be, and cherish each moment as it is truly a moment in which you are creating. You create the things you say, the things you do, the places you go, the people you associate with and as a result, you create your reality. Your actions and the thoughts that are prevalent in your mind are equal to your well being, and how you define and handle situations is how you retain your positive consciousness.

When you communicate with others, believe it or not, how you feel, and your attitude towards life, are expressive upon the lines on your face. When you think that you have hidden your anger and frustrations before, now you will realize why others that where positive had kept their distance from you in the past. When you find yourself surrounded by negative people, most likely you yourself are negative as well. Love, happiness, and compassion are feelings that you should become close friends with, as soon as you do, your reality will shift towards positive people and positive circumstances. Whenever you find your mind going astray, find a place in your mind that diffuses the negative energy. Each day you will have to test yourself, negative situations will occur, but how you handle the disposition in your mind is how you let it affect you.

The universe, and the ever flowing energy which is abundant around us, is a too that you have at your disposal, the thoughts that exist in your mind are the fulcrur and the foundation for the energy that you compose your life with. When you communicate with others do you seek to control of the situation or do you reciprocate energy in which is communicated to you? The control patterns that exist within an average conversation are apparent if you choose to open up and le your preconceived thought patterns slip away. If you choose to take control of a conversation without the reciprocation of energy and thought pertaining to the subject at hand, you will not be a good communicator. By taking control, or tryin to it will leave you in a state that will make you feel as though people do not wan to talk to you. When you communicate at the level of deceit and manipulation, yo cannot truly flourish as an individual. When you operate at the frequency of deceit, you can only expect to get deceit and manipulation from others.

Each day, each hour, each minute, and every second, are opportunities, moment in which you can paint your reality, mold your future, and become in each moment, who you would like to be. The nature of a spiritual being is to manifest your dreams as realities and your belief and faith are the composites of doing so. When you fear or doubt that you can have, do, or achieve, you are essentially telling yourself that you can't, and when you tell yourself that you can't, you can't. Can you? This is the question that you must ask yourself if you want to free yourself from your self-restrictive thought patterns.

The fact is that everything in the universe is built of subatomic particles and is composed molecularly in a certain fashion to hold a certain image. Every particle is joined on a microscopic level and without a certain structure it could not be bound together. The human body is composed of Oxygen, Carbon, Hydrogen, Nitrogen, Sulfur, Phosphorus, and a small percentage of other elements; 55 to 78 percent of our bodies are made of water. Our thoughts and actions also control our physical appearance and our overall health. As spiritual beings, our physical and mental framework can only function properly with the abundance of these minerals. Despite our internal health our soul stays intact, but it is necessary that we nourish our bodies with the right nutrients on a daily basis in order to function properly while we live on the physical plane. We are eternal beings and our reality only exists because we say it does, the great design is a construct of our mental status. Becoming a master of consciousness entails the deliverance of a poor mindset and becoming open to the infinite possibilities that the universe has to offer.

This equation may seem complex, but only by your definition of complex. Your understanding can only be expanded by your willingness to expand the spiritual superstructure of your mind and you may meet or exceed any level of intelligence if you wish to do so. Finding the elements of your thoughts that may create the lack of understanding, this is the key to spiritual, mental and physical enlightenment. Like tuning a musical instrument, the music can only be played harmoniously if it is well tuned, symbolically this is now shall tune your life, each string of your life must be tuned properly in order to meet your own personal state of harmony. Figure out what parts of your life are out of tune, then work on tuning each segment until you can strike a chord and make your destinies a reality.

Fundamentally, you know what you want, but some of us have lost our sense of consciousness. Life and its endless tests can leave you empty and unwilling to put effort to certain tasks, but it is through these times where we gain strength and knowledge. Your ideal place on earth is your ideal piece of mind and deciding how to acquire that inner peace is like a chemical formula that is unique to every individual. What kind of earthly situations are you trying to work through? How would this make your existence on this planet a more peaceful one? All the answers you will ever need are stored within and complexly you are the only one who could find the questions that are in accord with the things that you are seeking in life.

Should you try to become a better person, you must first find a greater level of consciousness that works in harmony with your personal circumstances. We all have a different set of dilemmas that we all have to strive to work through and in the process there is a set of lessons to be learned. Your ability to filter out the energy in which does not necessarily circulate well within your mind is all you have to do to start your accelerated movement in consciousness. With a high level of consciousness, your tendency to overcome obstacles becomes like a walk in the park, a situation that does not hinder your development, but acts as a method or some type of exercise in the learning process.

When you decide that each event in life is a lesson and the events that occur in your overall life are pieces of knowledge, everyday becomes a dream in which you hold the link between thought and reality. Paint a picture in the sky, be colorful, and manifest your true meaning in life as though it already exists. Your imaginational influence holds all the elements that you need to patent your ideals and dreams and while doing so you can operate at the plane of diversity that you wish function.

Choosing your thoughts and actions correctly is the operative tool in leading a healthy lifestyle. Even the smallest amount of negativity can grow into a demon, thus, affecting your life in a way in which you feel depleted. If you have the constant feeling of being ineffective, most likely you are and it probably resonates in all avenues of your life. The energy connected to ineffectiveness, is that of laziness, or the energy of incompletion, the answer to this equation is to follow through with what you want to do, and resolving any barriers that step in your path. Having the feeling of doubt is closely related to the amount of faith that you have, by having a stronghold of knowing that there are a multitude of possibilities, this may side-step your hesitance to have faith. The constant feeling of hate is a very strong emotion and the energy that hate is rooted from is your own harsh judgment, or self-hatred, if you don't like yourself, how can anyone else like you?

These feelings in addition to the many others may seem to be caused by external forces but can only be found from within. By becoming conscious of all the different things that may be affecting your life you may become the master of your reality and the molder of your universe. Without having self-awareness, you cannot have a conscious realization of what is truly going on in your life or even have a clue as to how to repair what it is that you must.

Learning how to coexist with the people around you, understanding the energy that they possess, and how to block the negative forces that are among them, are things that you must adhere to you consciousness. Being able to deflect the bad energy and absorb the positive energy is your route to a higher consciousness. This road can be as short or as long as you want and people may think that you are strange, but above all, the judgments of others shouldn't play a part in your reality the more they do, the slower your growth will become, and the lower frequency you will be operating on.

How many times do you think, "What will such and such think?" This is a habit that many of us are not aware of and we often get disappointed by the response of others as the result of it. Why do we hold so much weight on the thoughts of others, and why do we let it run our lives? Think of how you would feel if you were happy on your own terms regardless of what others felt about you, how freeing would that be? There is only importance in pleasing yourself, and when you do, you will find that others with the same philosophy on life will move in to your social surroundings because it just always works that way. People always seek those who are like them without necessarily knowing it. At each stage of advancement, your social structure will also advance. It's like Hitler hanging around with Jesus, it just wouldn't happen. Keep a keen eye on those which you surround yourself with, they may just be a perfect reflection of you?

Our physical life is a symphony of thoughts, realities, and actions, all of which dance together in a synchronistic pattern, a pattern which is formulated by our consciousness and conducted by our minds and the thoughts that prevail. The music that plays is our reality and the results that we manifest are coordinated by our actions. What kind of music will you write? Let the music play, sing your lifetime conquest as though you are manipulating the universe at each moment and find in life what you had only thought of in your dreams.

Part 8

*

No matter how much one may think that they do not have an ego, it is crucial to understand that we all do, some of us more, and some of us less. When you believe that you do not, your ego is actually telling you that you do not, but in reality, you do. Learning how to understand how your ego operates is a fundamental element in the process of expanding your consciousness and finding one's true self. You see people all the time, the ones that think they are right all the time, the people who can't take no for an answer, people who try to control situations as though they are the only ones who can figure it out. There are long lists of things that people do that are attached to egoism in many degrees of intensity.

Understanding the factors involved in being run by ego is a crucial step towards your growth. Ego is roadblock in your personal development and the stronger it is; the further your development must go. It can be the single most important thing to overcome, and maybe the hardest. You cannot completely rid of your ego, but you can develop an awareness that tones it down to a manageable level. Control, anger, judging others, self-righteousness, and deception are all areas within ego and while nobody wants to have these unfavorable characteristics, they may become abundant if not controlled properly.

The only person that you can truly control effectively is yourself and how you do that is up to you, just make sure it's towards a positive virtue and the end-results are for self benefitting. Sometimes people can control themselves in a destructive manner leading to all kinds of problems in their lives, or shall I say lack of control. Think about what you say to yourself, and think about what you say to others and you will catch yourself saying and doing things that you never really noticed were self defeating. In this day and age, from the outside looking in, we look as though we are a self-destructive society, so we eat processed foods, smoke tobacco, drink alcohol, and take prescription drugs, and do other things to harm our bodies and our minds. It's almost if we give up in a certain way, but these substances will not harm us in the short term, so in fact we tend to think that they are harmless, thus creating cancers and disease of every kind. Our ego tells us that these things won't harm us, the factors that create these thoughts are all based on the manipulation via advertisements which are done on psychological studies and the fact that most people indulge in these substances, and we have the feeling that it is ok. Balance would be the word to describe how you should handle your egotistical control factors, and your consciousness must be ready on many different levels if you want to grow indefinitely.

On the basis of those who think they know everything and force their control upon others to get things done, they are in fact practicing the strongest form of self defeat. Once you have convinced yourself that you know everything, or have the answer to every situation, you have stopped the life train and can only move even further into your ego once you get to this point. You have met people that are compulsive liars, and these people are often the people who have the idea that they know everything. When you think you have to be right all the time, you begin to fabricate your responses and have the tendency to pose your thoughts as truth, when in actuality there is no factual evidence to back up what they have said. Do you know a person like this? Are you this person? Some of you may be this person and without first analyzing who and what you stand for, you cannot truly find what it is that is disabling your livelihood.

You must ask yourself a handful of questions in order to find your egotistical characteristics, and sometimes you may even lie to yourself, this is very common. We often lie to ourselves so we can feel better about what we are doing. This is a subconscious action that we must move into our consciousness if we want to become aware of it. Restrain yourself from becoming too comfortable, you are actually holding yourself back and when you feel comfortable all the time and you are most likely taking the easy way out. When you practice doing the things that you don't necessarily feel comfortable doing, you are expanding your mind to new places. Often you will think, "Why didn't I try doing this before?" When you do this, you are actually reprogramming your mind into new thought processes, and when you start to learn new processes, you are exercising your mind as you should. When your mind becomes stagnant, you become the person that knows everything, and that is not the person that you want to become or continue being.

Make a habit of doing things that you would normally do, different, as long as your mind is working, you are growing, and when you are growing, you are learning. When you systemize your life, everything begins to become a repetitious set of actions and thoughts, and when one thing starts to fall out of order people often can't handle their reality. By making a habit of doing things differently, your mind will build a network of mental patterns where it creates chemicals that furnish the aptitude to troubleshoot the problems that may exist. Not only will your mind become stronger, but your ability to figure things out will become simpler.

Like a train on a set of tracks going to and from the same two locations, your mind, if systemized in a way that you always do the same things, can hinder your progression in life. This is why you see more people doing what they don't want to do, complaining about just about everything, dissatisfied with every aspect of their life. When people see everyone doing something, it becomes very easy to emulate what others are doing instead of following your own desires, "Hey, such and such is doing it". Those same people, when you do decide to do something out of the ordinary, try to bring you down to their level. How do we deflect the opinions of those in our immediate surroundings? This is when you have to decide what it is that you want to do and what it is that you want to be. Nobody really has the say in what you become in your life except you.

When you lack the sense of belief, it is usually because someone in the past told you that you cannot. These people, in all aspects, can be the worst possible people to surround yourself with, especially if you live with them. Maybe the best possible option is to avoid that type of communication with them. Most of the time, when we have a great idea, or a thing that we want to explore, we go those in our personal surroundings to give us moral support. We often take whatever people say too seriously and change our minds about the things that we want to do because of them. Isn't it us that really has the say in what we want to do?

If this is your personal reality, you must not communicate these things with those particular people. Show yourself that you can do these things, impress yourself, make yourself happy, without your own internal belief you can't enjoy your life or pursue the things that you aspire to. We all need communication, we all need support to a certain degree, but you must find those that truly support you, beyond this, please don't do something only if you have the support of others, sometimes you have to go with your intuition, follow the path that your mind has built for you. Start to follow the signs and clues that are given to you by your instinct. If it doesn't feel right, then don't do it, but don't let others curve your thoughts in a way that immobilizes you.

Inner strength comes from drive and determination and can only be hindered by you, outer forces will pound at your door, but you cannot let them in. Be a soldier of glory, stand tall and defeat those who wish to bring you down. Be the light that shines the string of hope when you are at the end of your rope, the barricade to those who do not believe in you, a hero, and the savior of your own reality.

The truth, and the ability to believe, lives within your soul, it's the energy that electrifies your existence and puts a positive flow on your daily life as well as the choices and actions that you decide to make. Retrieve the anchor that you have set forth, and sail away, look into the distance and see the future ahead of you, do not look back, blind your eyes from seeing what is behind you, it has only brought you forward and has become the test that you have passed to make you who you are today, learn a new day, a new way to say that you have played the game the way that you should without regret.

Get your juices flowing, take a deep breath and embark on a new mission, a voyage into the unknown, make each day a day to live to the fullest potential, draw a map to your treasure in the sky, and then follow the path. We sometimes forget who we are despite the hustle and bustle of life, how do we retain our inner move-forward mechanism? How do we find balance among those who surround us? Ask yourself,

"Who am I?"

Then answer the question within, be accountable for all your thoughts and actions, and know that you are the one who designs the life that you are living. Don't let the outer workings of society play a role in your life, unless it flows directly with your desires. You must keep an eye out for the things that present themselves. When you put your energy into the manifestation of your desires, the universe will work with you as a partner in creativity, but without the right degree of consciousness, you will not see the sign, the door to your ideals and aspirations.

Make a pact with yourself to not let anyone undermine the thoughts and feelings that you store within your heart. Don't let anyone weaken your desires with jealousy, envy, or disrespect. Who are you? Why would you let anyone kill your newborn dreams and desires?

Believe it or not, some feed on the pity of others, when they get fed, they want more. When you let them get the best of you, you are feeding their ego. Why not let them starve and face their own harsh reality? Disconnection from these people will make them look within to find what it is that is actually ailing them. Everyone holds goodness, but the willingness to show these characteristics become shadowed by the lack of self esteem and the abuse from others. These people are in your life for a reason and your job is, to find out what this reason is.

We often find ourselves coping with these outer forces instead of dealing with them, and the fact of the matter is that we must be the beacon of light that shines beyond the negative people in our lives. Put your cards on the table and deal with whatever you must. If you don't bring yourself to awareness regarding these things, you will not grow in the way, or even at the pace at which you want your life to operate.

Finding the anchor in which you become grounded may be as difficult as tying your shoes, but for some it may be as difficult as rocket science. You're the one in which controls the speed at which you can supersede your ego or at least get a handle on it. Some may feel as though there is an excuse for every experience that they are confronted with rather than knowing that everything is just and that we are meant to experience every experience that we are dealt with. When you blame you or someone else you become the one who operates with a lack of accountability and disregard for the experiences that are meant to be a learning process.

These experiences in your life are the daily tests that you must pass in order to be in the spectrum of growth in which you are meant to be in. Having a sensitivity or awareness is truly your connection to your soul and the meaning in life. The meaning in life is not to follow the lead of others, but to listen and absorb the experiences that occur in your lifetime. Each day there are a set of meaningful adventures that keep the intuition exercised, it is your job to digest what each event means and how you can grow, not how easily it can defeat you.

Thinking positive alone will not guarantee a way out of your present circumstances. Although you must remain positive in your daily adventure, you must act on your intuition as well as understand that you cannot build your dreams in a day, it is a step-by-step process in which you start by building a good foundation. With a strong foundation, you can build beautiful castles in the sky, an anchor for the truth that lies within, a self portrait in which all you have to do is color by number. You're entirely capable of becoming whatever it is that you aspire to, all you have to do is visualize the end result and fill in the blanks as you move forward.

The secret within is not a secret at all, it is the glory of God that lives inside, the creative force that runs through all of us. In the process of expanding your soul, you will undergo a transformation, a transmutation of spirit into the physical realm, and you will ultimately find the oneness which lies within the infinite universe that surrounds us.

Your inner-connectivity is dependent upon how much of your physical being in which you are able to sacrifice to your spiritual being. The physical realm is only a set of visuals that hold definitions, definitions that you create for individual objects. Your harsh judgments and thoughts toward things are what create your physical reality. Your soul speaks in momentum, energy, operating on a wavelength that is equal to your mental construct. If you think on something certainly, and definitely, the manifestation of something equal in energy and bearing on your soul is likely to materialize. You don't always get exactly what you think about, but you will always find something equal in capacity that will show itself to you in your reality. It's all about how you define experience, this is the key to creating your reality. By definition, I mean that you must also be very sensitive to signs or omens that will lead you in the right direction, if you fail to make yourself aware of these particular omens, you will not be likely to find it is that you are looking for, hence, if you are not looking, you will not find.

*

Rejoicing with your inner spiritual power is a process, an endless process that you can never master, even the spiritual masters of the past were aware of these concepts and you mustn't deny the fact that you are never done with growing, learning and expanding your consciousness, there will always be more room to grow, no matter how advanced your conscious awareness may become, you can always grow further.

Throughout history, there have been teachers and spiritual masters that have lived by these principles and this book is dedicated to the continuation and mastery of these concepts to enable a prosperous future for mankind itself in the years to come.

Although in my lifetime I have lived through some tremendously adverse circumstances of my own demise, I have been able to become the creator of my reality through the concepts described in this book. As a child I was unfortunate to be the product of a single-parent family, my mother, though uneducated, did her best to raise both my sister and I with the greatest of her power. My father, a man dedicated to a life of crime had no part in my development as a person has spent the majority of his life in prison that is the byproduct of his thoughts and actions.

As a person often uses the tools prescribed to them by their parents, I was gifted with not having any moral support. You are probably asking yourself why I said "gifted". I used the term gifted because without moral support, I had the opportunity to become curious of many different aspects of life. Although it may have been difficult and an arduous task, these aspects, in which I used trial and error to accommodate into my life, are some of the most important things that led me to be who I am today.

From trial and error, the fundamental tool of learning, I was able to use what I had experienced as a person, to build a set of guidelines in which I used to maintain a foundation that kept an always transforming ground under my feet despite the circumstances.

Through my journey in life, even though the experiences may seem quite extreme, I lived without a smidgeon of fear, which led to a life of uncertain results in which led to drug abuse, alcoholism, imprisonment, poverty, and self-abuse. Until I had found faith and a diverse understanding of spirituality, psychology, and quantum physics, I was on a meaningless path, a path that the majority of people lead, and a life with the mentality that life just happens.

Even though I have been on the bottom of the barrel several times, what had made me weak before that now empowers me today. Not to say that you have not had a life of the same circumstances, these are the things that have built my strength within. We all have our story which is why I chose not to dwell on the events of the past in the pages in this book. My fire within, the driving force that pushes me forward was built upon my ability to dissolve the things that had once led my life. My path has brought me to this point, and the pages in this book are meant to be a guiding light for those who have once been lost as well. No matter how deep you have dug a ditch for yourself, there is always a way out, a better path in which you can take. Farewell, and happy trails my friends. Expand your soul and always move forward.

The End

Stay tuned for more books on the Expansion of the Soul.

Go to http://www.willbarnesonline.com for more info.

www.ingramcontent.com/pod-product-compliance
Lightning Source LLC
LaVergne TN
LVHW021507080426

835509LV00018B/2425